Child Guidance
Through Play

Child Guidance Through Play

Teaching Positive Social Behaviors (Ages 2–7)

Charles H. Wolfgang

Florida State University

Boston   New York   San Francisco
Mexico City   Montreal   Toronto   London   Madrid   Munich   Paris
Hong Kong   Singapore   Tokyo   Cape Town   Sydney

Series editor: *Traci Mueller*
Editorial assistant: *Krista E. Price*
Manufacturing buyer: *Andrew Turso*
Senior marketing manager: *Elizabeth Fogarty*
Cover designer: *Suzanne Harbison*
Production coordinator: *Pat Torelli Publishing Services*
Editorial-production service: *Stratford Publishing Services*
Electronic composition: *Stratford Publishing Services*

For related titles and support materials, visit our online catalog at www.ablongman.com.

Between the time Website information is gathered and then published, it is not unusual for
some sites to have closed. Also, the transcription of URLs can result in unintended
typographical errors. The publisher would appreciate notification where these errors occur so
that they may be corrected in subsequent editions.

Library of Congress Cataloging-in-Publication Data

Wolfgang, Charles H.
　　Child guidance through play : teaching positive social behaviors (ages 2–7) / Charles Wolfgang.
　　　　p.　　cm.
　　Includes bibliographical references and index.
　　ISBN 0-205-36660-0
　　1. Play. 2. Early childhood education. 3. Child development. 4. Behavior modification.
I. Title.

　　LB1139.35.P55W64　2004
　　15.4'18--dc21　　　　　　　　　　　　　　　　　　　　　　　　2003050293

Printed in the United States of America

10　9　8　7　6　5　4　3　2　　　　　07　06　05

CONTENTS

v

PREFACE

This book is for the preschool teacher or caregiver who works with children ages two to seven in group settings. The teacher will become empowered to deal not only with the small misbehaviors typically seen in young children but also with the behaviors of the more difficult child. This text will focus more specifically on those children in our classrooms who bite, hit, spit, and "pepper" both the adult and their peers with swearing, bathroom talk, and their clear defiance, disrupting activities and at times endangering others. In contrast stands the child who is flat, expressionless, and hard to reach. These children make it difficult for teachers to get involved in or excited about the learning activities that they are providing.

Aggressive, passive, and very difficult children are the ones who keep teachers awake at night, worrying about how to help them and how to keep others safe from their actions. *Child Guidance Through Play* gives concrete teacher strategies for dealing with such children. The strategies suggested reject a reward-and-punishment discipline or behavioral philosophy—*children are never punished or rewarded*. The guidance provided for these difficult children recognizes the stages and phases, a developmental railroad track, of social-emotional development that all children must travel as they grow to maturity. My position is that these difficult children are stalled along this developmental track; they may be ages four or five, but their behavior is more characteristic of the toddler or two-year-old.

Aggression is defined here simply as *energy misdirected*. The difficult child must first be bonded to both a caring adult (the teacher) and his peers, thus enabling him to find a place in a social community. Then, through teacher guidance, the child learns to channel his or her aggression into productive play activities. To accomplish this, the classroom must be developmentally appropriate, containing such play items as blocks, Legos, and puzzles, and such fluid expressive materials as paint and clay. Most important, there must be an abundance of props and space for dress-up fantasy play, or sociodramatic play. These basic play materials will be used to challenge the child to develop the social skills that will serve him in later formal schooling and in life.

Acknowledgments

I wish to express a very warm "thank you" to Jeanne C. Meliori for her hard work and enthusiasm for this project. I'd also like to thank the following reviewers for their helpful comments on the manuscript: Jan Allen, University of Tennessee; Georgianna Duarte, University of Texas, Brownsville; Alice Honig, Syracuse University; and Adena Sexton, University of New York at Buffalo.

INTRODUCTION

Tracy, the aggressive, "hit-back-first" child:

Tracy was a slightly overweight preschool girl who often struck, pushed, kicked, and, at times, bit other classmates. During the first days at the preschool, Tracy engaged in these aggressive activities, directing such violence at anyone, including some teachers, if they unknowingly wandered near her. She appeared to have a defensive bubble around her of four to five feet. If others invaded this bubble, she appeared to feel threatened, and this triggered her aggression. Normally, the child who was attacked was completely innocent and meant her no harm, and Tracy's aggressive actions were unprovoked. To the teacher, she was like a grenade that could explode for no real reason. Tracy expected others to hurt her. From her fearful view of the world, she tended to "hit back first"* as a form of self-protection.

In the block corner, Tracy was constantly destroying block towers that she or any nearby child had constructed. She latched onto the alligator in the miniature life toys and had it beat up all the dolls and baby animals. Similarly, Tracy's art projects contained all of the available materials that she could pile onto them. Her paintings, both finger and brush paintings, degenerated into smeary messes, even to the extent that her fingers or the brush would tear holes in the paper. Her collages were normally covered with layers of flaking paste and a collection of materials that she could not name or that did not express any symbolism or meaning.

Snack time, which required her to be confined to a chair in close physical proximity to her peers, would produce aggressive behavior from her, such as grabbing all of the cookies and preventing others from getting their share. Tracy could never relax at rest time; she rocked constantly as she sucked her thumb, or she would masturbate, or at times she would fill the room with guttural sounds that disturbed her neighbors as they attempted to sleep or rest.

Larry, the highly introverted and nonexpressive, helpless child:

Larry was a small, thin child with an automatic nervous smile that he used in responding to any intrusion, such as overtures by peers or requests by teachers. He came into the preschool on the first day holding his body rigid and looking around as little as possible. His favorite spot was a lone chair next to the record player, which he watched spin; he would often look off into space for long periods of time.

Larry rarely used language except when questioned or prodded by his teachers. When he could not put a puzzle or a manipulative toy together, he would just sit with it in front of him, making no motion to seek help or to try another solution. He

---

*Nancy Curry, personal communication

appeared to live in a dream world. When the other children had snacks, Larry often had to be persuaded to eat; otherwise, he would eat nothing at all. At rest time, he delighted in shutting his eyes and lying quite still. His mother reported that at home when she scolded him, he ran to his room and fell asleep on his bed.

Larry's favorite art activities were coloring with crayons and magic markers. During these activities, he would visually check the adult's response for signs of approval or disapproval. Larry hated finger painting and water play. His first response to these experiences was to call out "No, no, no!" while holding himself rigidly.

In the dress-up corner, Larry's participation consisted only of being dragged in by some of the bossier children and made the "baby" or "prisoner" or another character with whom they could do what they wanted; even then, he couldn't maintain this play.

At home, Larry was the younger of two children. His mother valued the early "mothering role" and enjoyed his babyish needs and behaviors. This loving family was against "strict punishment" and set few firm limits against which Larry would have to rebel.

Tracy and Larry depict the types of preschool children who have difficulty in taking advantage of an early school experience, but who, more than anyone, need positive classroom experiences. There are other children, far in the majority, who actively engage in their preschool world and at a later date seem to fit smoothly into elementary school with its demands for developing formal skills such as reading, writing, and arithmetic. But it is with the former, the aggressive and passive two-, three-, four-, five-, and six-year-olds like Tracy and Larry, that we are concerned. These children have neither the ability nor the commitment to master their world and to control their impulses, nor do they have the freedom to take risks in a dynamic preschool setting. They appear stalled in their growth towards acquiring and mastering new social skills. It is the purpose of this book to describe practical constructs that may be used to view the growth of such children. We will also present techniques for stimulating such difficult children with the use of play as a vehicle towards cognitive and emotional development (Saltz, Dixon, & Johnson, 1977).

REFERENCE

Saltz, E., Dixon, D., & Johnson, J. (1977). Training disadvantaged preschoolers on various fantasy activities: Effects on cognitive functioning and impulse control. *Child Development, 48*, 367–380.

1

Understanding Aggressive, Passive, and Very Difficult Behaviors

The young child is born helpless into this world, and he* exists and grows within the protective, caring "shell" of his mother or other significant adults. It is this care that screens out the harsh world and provides the needed stimulation, food, warmth, and love that helps to protect the maturing infant (Ainsworth, 1995; Erikson, 1963; Mahler, 1970; Mahler, Pine, & Bergman, 1975; Spitz, 1965; Sroufe & Cooper, 1999) as the child psychologically hatches into the social world. While in this protective shell, the child can maintain an inner emotional security, thus enabling him to use his energies for active play and growth experiences. Through this caring, young children acquire a basic trust in their world and in their own abilities to get their needs met and to solve daily, normal frustrations (Erikson, 1963). When this protective shell cracks prematurely, leaving the child to fend for himself before he has the physical, cognitive, and emotional skills to do so, or when the child is not permitted to begin the separation process because of overprotectiveness, then the child's emotional development is stunted. The Introduction describes children like Tracy and Larry, who retreat to the defensive positions of ritualistic behaviors, either aggressive or passive, that are nonproductive for their growth. During the first three years of life, most well-functioning young children make major steps in gaining autonomy and adaptability as they become aware of themselves as competent individuals and separate from the caring parent (Mahler, 1970; Mahler et al., 1975).

Child development researchers (Ainsworth, 1995; Erikson, 1963; Mahler, 1970; Mahler et al., 1975; Spitz, 1965; Sroufe & Cooper, 1999) have now shown how the separation process occurs. The infant attaches to significant adults who daily care for him and then gradually begins breaking free from the dependency. As a toddler and preschooler, he becomes an independent, competent, social being who is able to work and play with others in a cooperative manner while maintaining an inner emotional stability and confidence. When teachers see children like aggressive,

---

*In this book, the masculine pronoun is used to identify the child (unless otherwise specified) and the feminine pronoun for the teacher; but obviously both girls and boys have developmental difficulties in preschool, and many preschool teachers are male.

hostile Tracy or passive, introverted Larry in the preschool classroom, they hypothe-size that something has disrupted the normal developmental process. The aggressive and passive preschoolers do not have the inner emotional security to actively play and problem solve (Gottman, 1977).

Aggressive children are stalled in a position of hostility or defensiveness. All of their energies are used to defend themselves emotionally with little or no free energy to use for growth experiences. These children frighten, challenge, and defeat their teachers, who protect their students and themselves from the childrens' aggressive acts. Deep feelings toward such aggressive children are ones of fearfulness (Dreikurs, Grunwald, & Pepper, 1989). On the other hand, the passive, introverted child does not make immediate demands for daily intervention, but teachers realize in quiet moments that they feel inadequate to help them (Dreikurs et al.).

Understanding this social-emotional hatching process as a universal track on which most normal children progress can help teachers develop strategies that are appropriate in setting limits and intervening with such difficult children. These strategies will provide direction for the child in acquiring new behaviors over many days, months, or years that finally lead the child to appropriate development.

The Four "Worlds"

Consider how adults retreat back through these phases, or "worlds," as a result of traumatic life experiences. Suppose your beloved pet has been injured, and you are required to take immediate action. You act on reflex, applying cloth and compres-sion to the wound to stop the blood flow, picking up the pet, and rushing it to the animal hospital. You enter a busy waiting room with pet in arms.

World 4: Language and the Social Self

You explain to the receptionist what has occurred and request immediate care for your suffering pet. If you do not have your needs met and get off-putting responses such as "There are two people ahead of you" or "We are not able to deal with you at this moment," your emotional tensions increase because of a sense of danger to your beloved pet. You try again to get help through language and reasoning, but again without success. A fully functioning person, or a child as he matures, needs to func-tion in a social world with others and get his needs met by communication through language with others. When adults cannot get these needs met, we begin to regress, retreating back to less mature phases or worlds—much like a fight-or-flight response.

World 3: Verbal Aggression and the Outside Self

You begin to feel the adrenaline pumping through your body and the blood rushing to your face. Your hands begin to sweat, and you begin to "snap and snarl" at the receptionist, using verbal aggression and even threatening statements: "Somebody deal with me here! I want to see the doctor now, not tomorrow! If this animal dies, you're going to have a lawsuit on your hands! I want help now, darn it!" Because of your emotional state, you still have the intellectual capacities to deal with the outside world but now have regressed to verbal aggression out of a growing sense of helplessness. With continued or increased frustration, you may retreat still further, to physical aggression.

World 2: Physical Aggression and the Body Self

You are now even more panicked or emotionally flooded, and you become physically aggressive as you pound on the receptionist's glass window to get her attention, possibly grabbing at her by the arm or shirt to turn her around to face your direction, making her attend to your words. You may even kick at the locked door to the doctor's office, while still holding the pet in your arms. Most likely you become so emotionally flooded that you are no longer rational but are simply reacting, overwhelmed by your emotions and the adrenaline pumping through your brain and body—you are animal-like and in a physically aggressive fight stance.

World 1: Passivity and the Inside Self

When the pet is taken away and you are left behind to wait, you retreat into your Inside Self. Perhaps later that evening, you begin to relive the traumatic happenings of the day, experiencing the fear, guilt, and anger. You think about how you might have acted differently and more effectively. You feel guilty about your own verbally and physically aggressive behavior and you feel depressed about the day's occurrences.

Hypothetically, this example shows that we live in four worlds: the Inside Self, full of thoughts and feelings that are both positive and negative; the Body Self, where we are unthinking, reactive beings, using physical acts to attempt to get our needs met; the Outside Self, where we employ verbal aggression or intimidation; and finally, the Social Self, where we are able to use language and thoughts to work cooperatively with others and get our needs and wants met in a responsible manner.

Adults suffer these normal daily life experiences and regress through these worlds, but normally they will quickly bounce back, returning to the Social Self where they can work effectively and comfortably with others. The ability to bounce back and not be immobilized and depressed by such life experiences is called *ego strength*. Children under age three do not have the established ego strength that adults have, and they may not have the ability to bounce back. Because of a traumatic incident, they get stuck developmentally in one of these worlds. A child may retreat to the passive world of the Inside Self where he is flooded by emotions, reliving fearful events, appearing withdrawn in a sleeplike state, and even beginning to behave destructively toward himself, such as pulling out his hair, striking his head against a wall, or biting his hands or body until he bleeds. The young child could be stuck in the physically aggressive world of the Body Self, where he simply responds aggressively to any or all demands and intrusions with assaultive behaviors, such as grabbing or striking. Others might get stuck in the verbally aggressive world of the

Outside Self, using hostile threats, swearing, bathroom talk, and defiance to defend themselves. Finally, there is the mature behavior of the child who can use language to express and get his needs met without aggression or helplessness, in the world of the Social Self (see Figure 1.1). Even when the child grows and matures to the world of the Social Self, and he works and plays with others, he will at times refuse to comply with adult requests by asking "Why?" questions as a diversion technique or by simply being negative about requests to comply and cooperate. It is in this world of the Social Self that the child learns to play with others.

This adaptive growth process—that is, the ability to come into a preschool classroom and to play and work cooperatively with others—requires the mastery of a multitude of encounters with varying degrees of stress as the child moves into a wider world and clashes with the limits that this world sets for him. Such repetitive encounters challenge the child both emotionally and cognitively and provide an avenue for him to become a socially adaptive being.

As an infant with effective parenting, a child is very powerful, needing only to give a small cry to get adults to begin an active process to determine what might be causing the infant's stress (needing to be fed, diapered, etc.). Adults care for these needs until the infant returns to a state of comfort and pleasure. Therefore, it can be said that the infant is born very powerful. Imagine if adults could vocalize their needs and the social world would spin around to serve them—this would truly make adults powerful!

But this balance of power suddenly changes once the infant becomes a toddler. Because the toddler can walk and run away from the protective shell of caring adults,

FIGURE 1.1   Passive-Aggressive Phases

Developmental phase	Level of hatching	Teacher's feeling toward the child
Language Vocal ▪ "Why" questions ▪ Negativity	Level 4: Social Self	Effective
Verbal aggression ▪ "No"/defiance ▪ Swearing/threats	Level 3: Outside Self	Annoyed or defeated
Physical aggression ▪ Strike ▪ Grab	Level 2: Body Self	Hurt
Passivity ▪ Self-destructive ▪ Sleeplike state	Level 1: Inside Self	Inadequate

adults now begin to teach him to care for himself through the setting of limits: "No, don't go near the step," "don't run into the street," and a host of other prohibitions. These prohibitions cause inner tensions that motivate the child to actively master the situation or problem. Such mastery is a gradual, developmental process. As the child becomes able to accept these "no's," he gains control of his own behavior. Impulse control can then be viewed as the product of a series of evolving phases (Spitz, 1957) that parallel the four worlds outlined here.

For example, the father comes in from having just chopped wood for the living room fireplace and, unthinkingly, lays the ax on the floor. The toddler immediately sees this new and interesting object in his world and he rushes to inspect it with his hands. The father, now realizing his mistake, physically intervenes, taking the ax away from the toddler and even possibly using the word "no." The toddler and later the more mature preschooler will handle this frustration and limit setting in different manners. The very young toddler's first immature response to limits is one of passivity, retreating into the Inside Self, the world of thoughts and feelings. This can be seen when he gets his foot caught in the rung of his crib or is being prohibited from throwing his food.

During the early months of infancy, nearly every one of the young child's needs was indulged; but as the child begins to mature, the world begins to ask him to delay this immediate gratification and socialize his behavior. Thus, the young child as a toddler is initially surprised and startled by these first societal demands. The phase of passivity quickly changes to one of physical aggression, or the world of Body Self. The child reflexively kicks, bites, and grabs or attacks the person or object that, to some degree, has frustrated him—father has taken away a new and potential play object, the ax. The toddler who attempts to explore his father's ax first becomes passive, putting his thumb into his mouth, appearing glassy-eyed. Then he physically attempts to climb a chair to get to the table and the ax for the second time. Again, his father stops him, taking him down from the chair and now placing the ax in a location far out of the child's reach. The toddler now may scream, kick, and throw objects at the father who has frustrated him by blocking his wants and needs.

With the child's increased maturity, physical aggression gradually gives way to verbal aggression ("I hate you, daddy!"), or the Outside Self. The aggressive "no" is characteristic of the three-year-old and can still be heard in the preschool years. (Parent: "Would you like to take your bath now?" Toddler: "No!" Teacher: "Would you like to pick up the blocks now?" Preschooler: "No!")

Mother discovers three-year-old Susie decorating the living room walls with a crayon, and, upon seeing her mother rapidly approaching, Susie shouts "No, no" at her mother. The verbal hurling of "no" indicates the beginning development of the mental permanency or memory of the prohibition. But at this early phase, it is still remembered after the act is committed and upon seeing the presence of the adult who has set the limit. This aggressive "no" signals that the child is identifying with those important adults in his life that he loves, and he is now trying to do what adults desire him to do. Soon the child will remember the prohibition or "can say no to himself" beforehand, thus obeying rules and identifying with the adult and becoming more adult-like in his behavior—he can keep himself safe.

Aggressive "no's" also expand to other forms of aggressive language such as name-calling, swearing, and bathroom talk during the preschool years. At first it may seem like a contradiction to accept that the child who is screaming "I hate you!" or "You're a poopy pants!" (Outside Self) at a peer who has just taken his toy is evincing a much more mature response than the preschooler engaged in an outward physical attack (Body Self). It is with increased intellectual capacity and experience with language that the child can later state, "That's mine. I was playing with it first. Give it back!" (Social Self). Problem solving through language with others presents the child with the most mature way of finding answers to his needs and problems in his world (see Figure 1.2).

Internalization of "no," which is the beginning for the young child of the development of a conscience and the attainment of impulse control, is a process that moves through general personality states paralleling the four worlds previously described: first, as passivity, where the child retreats into his Inside Self; from passivity to physical aggression, or the Body Self; from physical aggression to verbal aggression, or the Outside Self; and, finally, from verbal aggression to the Social Self, where the child can express his needs and wants through effective language and the search for an alternative, socialized solution.

It is generally during the first seven years of life that a child passes through these fundamental phases. Although once having attained a level of maturity, the child will, as do more mature children and even adults, display passive and aggressive forms of behavior, and, to a limited extent, these will be considered normal

FIGURE 1.2   Impulse Control as a Developmental Process

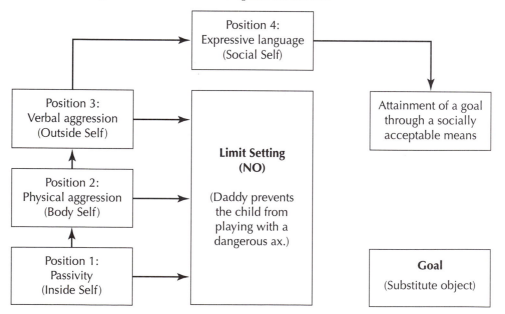

behavior. The setting of limits for young children by adults is not to be considered a punitive response by the adult, but rather a vehicle of caregiving, enabling the adult to balance a child's maturing capacities with the increasing demands of an expanding world. Setting limits helps keep the child safe, and the child begins to realize, when he does break rules and gets hurt, that he can depend on caring adults for safety.

For the purpose of this discussion, nonproductive young children, who have been described as physically and verbally aggressive or passive, are those who enter preschool unable to use the school experience productively and who demonstrate limited ability to play (Saltz, Dixon, & Johnson, 1977; Saltz & Johnson, 1974). Play is defined as the self-initiating activity of the child to express his ideas (Inside Self) through body actions (Body Self) and language (Outside Self) in cooperative activities with peers (Social Self). Thus, while playing, the child integrates all of the Selves described—play is the fully actualized, developmentally appropriate behavior for the preschool-age child.

In contrast to aggressive and passive children, consider four-year-olds Walter, Jane, and Kate, who have wandered into the dress-up area of the classroom. Walter places the doctor's stethoscope to his ears, dresses in the doctor's coat, and explores the doctor's satchel, containing small plastic replicas of doctor tools, including real bandages. Kate giggles as she watches Walter place the probing end of the stethoscope to Jane's chest and now joins the activity by first dressing in the nurse's outfit and all of its accoutrements. Simulating many actions that they have obviously seen in their own daily lives, they play for well over a half hour, with Jane enjoying the role of the patient, complaining about a host of aches and pains, while both Doctor Walter and Nurse Kate attend to her. This is sociodramatic play (Smilansky, 1968; Smilansky & Shefatya, 1990), highly sophisticated social activity that first begins in well-developing three-year-olds and reaches its full maturity by the age of six. It is this cooperative social activity that the aggressive and passive preschooler cannot perform and that can be used to help him obtain an appropriate level of development. The playing children use and express their thoughts and feelings (Inside Self) through body actions (Body Self), with gestures and symbolic actions (Outside Self), and finally with language, able to carry out highly social (Social Self) activities. In contrast to these well-functioning children, remember Tracy, the aggressive, hit-back-first child, and Larry, the highly restricted and nonexpressive child, in the opening example.

The Passive Child

The passive preschool child lives daily in his own world. This child can be characterized as aimless and lethargic, at times moving from place to place. He is difficult to arouse or even stimulate to show interest or enjoyment. At times he shows a hint of play, but the activity is repetitive (simply moving toys about). The passive child's facial expressions are dull, with little indication of alertness. When invited to try new things, he seems afraid to tackle any new tasks and usually drifts disinterestedly toward small structured materials (puzzles) at tables. Rarely does he play with blocks or carpentry tools, or perform activities that require self-assertion, and he appears to view the world through a fog. Cognitively he detects no order, system, or clarity to objects or events in his life and is unable to remember or name objects and events (Krown, 1969; Swallow, 2000). (See also Figure 1.3.)

The passive child either has not grown out of or has retreated into Position 1, the Inside Self (see Figure 1.1), living in a protective shell of helplessness (Dreikurs et al., 1989). He cannot make the world work for himself or be a productive agent. He appears perceptually detached from the actions about him, spending most of his time in his internal fantasy world of thought, possibly experiencing feelings of fear.

Krown (1969) describes the behavior of the typical nonproductive child as follows:

> Chaim fell off the swing and banged his head, which immediately became swollen. He didn't utter a cry, seemed unchanged, kept a bland expression on his face, and did not respond to the teacher's efforts to comfort him. (Krown, 1969, p. 32)

The passive child may be viewed as having retreated into a personality state where he is cut off cognitively and emotionally from his world and his own body (Body Self).

The young child during the early years of life begins to extend himself into his world through the various sense modalities of touch, smell, vision, or a combination of these. These tentacles into the outside world are used by the child to obtain information, which he assimilates into a meaningful relationship to understand his world. A child in a dangerous world, a child who is hit for touching or who is screamed at or shaken, lacks a basic sense of trust. The child believes that to touch is

FIGURE 1.3   Classroom Behaviors of Passive Young Children

- Lethargic
- Flat expression; appear dull and lifeless
- Rarely laugh and smile
- Have little to no attention span, and drift off into an inner world of thought
- Reject expressive materials such as paints or clay
- Cannot be coplayers with others
- Choose structured, predictable items such as simple puzzles and do them over and over, tending to hide behind the material
- When cuddled, do not cuddle back (they feel limp like a wet noodle)
- At times lose bowel and bladder control (unable to read their own inner body signal of need)
- Refuse to eat or choose a narrow range of foods that they find acceptable
- Wander about without direction
- May perform self-abusive activities such as pulling out small amounts of their own hair or biting their own skin or fingers
- Difficult to awaken after nap time
- May cover ears at all sounds (as if sound can hurt)
- May be found masturbating at various times during the day, especially during story time or on the cot at nap time
- Go unnoticed by peers

to expose himself to injury (this is called a *punished modality*) or to look directly at an adult is to be interpreted as intrusive—"Don't you look at me that way, young man." Many passive children (Inside Self) not only appear to be cut off from their own bodily senses (Body Self) but also appear as if they have been punished. At any unusual or strong sound, the passive child will cover his ears as if it is painful to hear. The child cannot sustain a look at the face of the adult, or his fingers and hands move nervously. He is not able to touch such dynamic materials as paints or water for water play. This may also be seen in the passive child's inability to eat at snack time. The teacher may ask whether such passive children have been punished through the various modalities (hearing, touch, etc.). Intervention will be needed to reestablish trust with the child so that he can look, touch, and hear with confidence. The overall feeling that these helpless children provoke in the teachers who work with them is one of inadequacy: "I seem not to be able to help this child no matter what I do. He rejects it."

The Physically Aggressive Child

The aggressive child, who can be considered to be slightly more advanced developmentally (see Figure 1.1) than the passive child, maintains himself in a general personality state of panicked hyperalertness. The aggressive child is constantly flooded by tension and anxiety, which are dispersed through acts of impassivity and heightened motor activity. His sense modalities are acutely aware, and he is constantly prepared to defend himself. A fellow classmate accidentally bumps him, and he strikes out in an aggressive manner. He appears revengeful to others. He thinks "This world is unsafe and will hurt me, and I must be on the alert to defend myself. I must hit back first before they hit" (see Figure 1.4).

Krown (1969) states:

> In spite of their usual apathy, at times [they] would react with surprising impulsivity. They would suddenly run away from or destroy something they were making if it were not going well; some would suddenly run. [The aggressive children] frequently exhibited scenes of impulsive behavior, such as throwing themselves on the floor and kicking and screaming when they had to accept restrictions [limits]. (Krown, 1969, p. 55)

The feeling provoked by the aggressive child in the teacher is one of possibly being hurt or fear of not protecting other children from injury.

The Verbally Aggressive Child

Verbal aggression (saying "no," swearing, screaming, bathroom talk, and threats) by the child may be seen as demonstrating a more developmentally mature behavior. The verbally aggressive child has the same defensive fears as the physically aggressive child, but he has moved to the use of language. Whereas the physically aggressive child may attack by striking or grabbing, the verbally aggressive child strikes out with

FIGURE 1.4   Classroom Behaviors of Aggressive Young Children

- In motion even when seated (arms and legs are still overly active)
- Pick up then quickly discard objects
- May run and chase, putting themselves in dangerous positions or disrupting the classroom (leaving the school grounds, climbing to the tops of shelves, or pulling the cap on the indoor water table) and forcing adults to run after them
- May dislike quiet (such as at rest time) and will fill the void with own voice or with tapping sounds that annoy others
- Run, never just walk, or walk stiffly like a robot as if using effort to stop and control themselves
- Facial expressions are serious and intense; eyes dart from one object to another without ability to focus
- Have quick and intense interest in new activities and appear to push to be first as if fearful they may not get a turn
- When activities require committed focus, they will state angrily "I can't" and go off to something new
- When peers accidentally bump them, they respond with "So and so hit (or hurt) me" and with physical or verbal aggression
- Describe and are convinced that others are trying to hurt them, especially other active children to whom they are attracted

- Will be aggressive toward others without provocation (so fearful that others will hurt them, they hit back first even when not hit)
- When using fluids (finger painting/water play), they lose control of the materials, or love fluids and water play and use materials over and over as if to practice control
- Eat ravenously at snack time and will hoard food as if they are not sure they will get enough
- Cannot relax to fall to sleep at rest time
- May be overly sensitive to stimuli—cannot meet adults eye to eye, cannot be touched (especially for cuddling), sounds trigger increased fear and motor action
- Are light sleepers
- Do not choose or enjoy structured materials (blocks/puzzles) that are demanding and require thought to complete
- When fearful or angry may "pepper" adults with strong, sexually aggressive words
- Get silly and uncontrolled in the toileting area and will urinate on others
- Are feared and rejected by peers
- Play power games with parent at arrival and departure times
- Cannot maintain themselves in groups (circle time, snack time) and will annoy or be aggressive toward peers

aggressive language that may challenge the teacher's power. He is defiant and may begin with a hostile "no I won't" response to the teacher, which is most characteristic. The child may exhibit other forms of verbal aggression, such as back talk, denial, blaming, accusing, insults, and profanity.

The verbally aggressive child seems to dig in his heels and is verbally defiant, challenging the adult's power and abilities to get cooperative actions from him. The teacher working with the verbally aggressive child feels defeated and angry. She may think, "He can't talk to me that way," and may be tempted to use various forms of punishment. The verbally aggressive child expects this punishment, and when it comes it confirms his negative view that others will take actions to hurt him and are not trustworthy.

Expressive Language

Finally, the child matures to the position that he can move developmentally beyond the use of verbal aggression to the effective use of language to express his needs and get the world to work for him. The child that needs a pair of scissors that is being used by a fellow classmate seated next to him can turn, face his peer, and ask, "May I use the scissors when you are done?" This simple ability to use language has moved the child out of a fight-or-flight stance to the people around him and has enabled him to work effectively with others.

The preschooler should be viewed on a continuum that parallels that of the internalization of impulse control (see Figure 1.2). When the child wants and approaches a goal and cannot reach it, the frustration he experiences to his blocked need causes him to react either productively with language and self-control or non-productively with verbal aggression, physical aggression, or passivity. Consider how a three-year-old who has not fully moved through the phases may regress back through these worlds.

> The three-year-old has just watched her mother bring in the groceries an hour before dinnertime. She notices the gallon of ice cream sticking out of the top of the bag.
>
> > CHILD (*in a polite and ingratiating voice*): "Mommy, may I please have some ice cream, huh, please?" (Position 4—Social Self, effective use of language)
> >
> > MOTHER: "No, not now dear. Mommy is going to make dinner, and it will spoil your appetite. You may have some ice cream for dessert after dinner."
> >
> > CHILD: "No-o-o! Now, mommy! I want ice cream now!" (Position 3—Outside Self, verbal aggression)
>
> The child climbs a chair and gets hold of the ice cream box from the counter and attempts to open it. Mother sees this and takes the box away. The child screams and kicks at her mother. (Position 2—Body Self, physical aggression)
>
> Mother slides the kitchen door open and gently pushes the child out of the door to her sandbox (Vinturella & James, 1987).
>
> We will now see this child "rehatch" from Inside Self to Body Self to Outside Self, and again to Social Self (see Figure 1.1).
>
> The child seats herself in the sandbox, sticks her thumb into her mouth (which she slowly chews on), pulls her hair with her free hand, and pouts, looking back at her mother, who is sorting groceries. (Position 1—Inside Self, passivity)
>
> The child continues to pout and scowl in the direction of her mother. (Position 1—Inside Self, passivity)
>
> She stands and walks slowly around the sandbox and stops to kick with full force at a sand bucket. (Position 2—Body Self, physical aggression)

She drops to her knees, squeezing sand between her fingers and shouting, "I hate you, mommy!" (Position 3—Outside Self, verbal aggression)

She now begins to play with the sand, looking at her work, then back at her mother, who is busy cooking and paying her no attention. Finally, she giggles victoriously, and she pretends to "eat" an "ice cream" cone that she has made out of moist sand and a cup. (Position 4—Social Self, expressive play language, obtains the goal, "ice cream," in a socially acceptable manner).

In this discussion of passivity, physical aggression, verbal aggression, and the effective use of expressive language, the starting point is the totally passive or totally aggressive child. However, younger children might demonstrate behavior typical of all four positions. It is not until a child is six or seven years of age that he has moved fully through these four worlds and shows quite mature behavior and impulse control. In fact, the attainment of solid impulse control as a cooperative worker is necessary for real readiness for formal first-grade schooling (Freud, 1974).

The difficult child daily behaves as passive and, with increased development, will be mostly passive with abbreviated periods of physical aggression and impulsivity. It may sound quite unreasonable, but the child that is extremely passive and highly inactive for a period of two or three months and then kicks out at a fellow classmate who has taken his toy is showing more mature behavior. The action moves the child out of a helpless position but of course is still not productive. The aggression is energy misdirected, but turned outward. The physically aggressive behavior will continue and increase; slowly, verbal aggression appears (such as swearing and threats). Again, this is behavior of increased maturity. Finally, the child becomes empowered with the use of expressive language and is able to give up attempting to deal with the world through passive or physically or verbally aggressive (flight-or-fight) behaviors. Expressive language involves two processes: language and play.

The previous example in which the three-year-old used mature language ("Mommy, may I please have some ice cream, huh, please?") is what is wanted in a maturing child, but children—and adults—cannot always get what they want in their daily lives. The young child has a built-in fantasy world that is seen in expressive play. The three-year-old retreats to her sandbox and through fantasy play victoriously makes an ice cream cone out of wet sand and a small cup and pretends to eat it.

A child's fantasy permits him to move from being a helpless victim to active play (Erikson, 1963; Freud, 1974; Peller, 1959) and to compensate for the anger produced by the "no" from mom. For the young child, emotional experiences and frustrations are felt so intensely, it is as if experiences are too large to comprehend. The child retreats to the fantasy world of play, where he can replay the experiences in fantasy over and over until the experience is digested and understood (Atlas & Lepidus, 1987; Axline, 1969; Peller, 1959). If we watch closely the themes of the fantasy play, we will see the many emotional experiences that the child attempts to master—for example, a positive but overwhelming birthday party, a frightening TV show, an injury, or feelings of being small and powerless in a world of powerful adults.

Passive or aggressive children who cannot play may have lost this capacity for self-healing and are only responding to many of life's mild frustrations with nonproductive fight-or-flight behaviors (Ianotti, 1978). Later chapters show how to teach children to play in ways that help them gain the ability to move from helpless passivity to active agent.

Again, it should be noted that even when the child has established excellent abilities to use language, there will still be emotional incidents in which he will regress for very short periods of time to those fight-or-flight behaviors and then bounce back to more mature behavior.

The Teacher As a Feeling Person

Teachers at times may find themselves responding in a similarly regressive manner; it is important to consider the teacher as a "feeling person." When teachers work with young children daily, their reward is seeing the children mature and develop. The passive or aggressive child presents a major challenge. When he does not respond to traditional guidance, the teacher feels the added pressure of keeping other children safe, the potential criticism from the parents of other children who may have been the target of the difficult child's aggression, and the sinking feeling that other children will begin behaving in a similarly aggressive manner. By understanding these initial reactions, the teacher can gain a conscious awareness of her feelings and learn to disengage from them. With the techniques that follow, she can empower herself to gain control over her own emotions and her feelings toward these difficult children. Finally, she can establish a plan for helping them.

The passive-helpless child evokes feelings of inadequacy (Dreikurs et al., 1989) in the teacher (see Figure 1.1). Warm, nurturing overtures are made through guidance, but the child rejects that help and, by his passive behavior, communicates that he wants to be left alone. It's as if he is saying, "Don't make demands on me. I am ineffective, and I wish to hide here behind my wall of helplessness." After many attempts to help him day in and day out, the teacher begins to feel inadequate. She thinks, "This is one child that I will never be effective in encouraging."

The aggressive, hit-back-first child makes the teacher feel hurt and defeated (Dreikurs et al., 1989). She attempts to respond firmly with the aggressive child, but with warmth and acceptance. The aggressive child may respond to positive overtures and guidance with escalating hostility—kicking, biting, hitting, and even spitting. The teacher feels that she has not given this aggressive child any reason to respond to her in such a hurtful manner. For a few seconds, she may even consider returning his aggression with a small degree of physical punishment so that he sees how it feels. The teacher needs to disengage from these retaliatory feelings to develop a rational plan for coping with the acting-out child.

The verbally aggressive child will evoke in the teacher feelings of being defeated and/or annoyed (Dreikurs et al., 1989). Verbal threats are hurled at the teacher like missiles, while sexual talk, swearing, and similar verbal aggression gets excessive attention from peers and all adults within hearing. Commanding the verbally aggressive child to stop such unacceptable language seems only to encourage the child to challenge the adult's power.

If the teacher is overwhelmed with feelings of inadequacy, she first must disengage from these feelings and realize that the children themselves are feeling helpless. These difficult children have developed these automatic or reflexive behaviors over time, and their actions are not personally directed at the teacher as an individual. The teacher must realize that these nonproductive behaviors are signals that these children need our help. The construct of impulse control as a developmental process gives a rational explanation for these behaviors. Teachers will be able to use many of the suggested techniques in the following chapters to deal with such children and facilitate healthy emotional development.

Causes of Aggressive or Passive Behavior

When a teacher sees acting-out behaviors in young children, her first tendency may be to look for a cause and place blame. She might direct blame toward the parents, wanting to fix something in the home. She tends to use a "spark plug" theory of development—for example, if a lawn mower runs badly, she looks for a part that is not functioning right. Let's say she finds a faulty spark plug, and changes it to make the lawn mower run smoothly again. Human development is much more complex than the spark plug analogy (Escalona, 1968). Searching for someone to blame or something to fix is nonproductive for the teacher because when all is said and done, the teacher still has difficult children in her classroom and must deal with them on a daily basis.

An exception, of course, is for the child who has a medical condition that can be cured or treated. One aggressive three-year-old child was hyperactive, aggressive to others, and abusive to himself. Through a medical examination it was discovered that the child had a 60 percent hearing loss in the right ear because of a blocked eustachian tube. The pressure and pain that he felt was much like what an adult might feel when flying in an airplane and being unable to clear the inner ear. A minor operation to place a small tube in the child's ear alleviated the problem. Through the use of play guidance techniques following the surgery, the aggressive behavior and the self-abuse was eliminated, and the child demonstrated age-appropriate social behavior.

Teachers are first encouraged to have a child receive a full medical examination when passive or aggressive behaviors are exhibited, to rule out any medical causes for such behaviors. Medical conditions can be found and treated before a play program of intervention in the classroom is started. A medical examination may be required as part of the school admission criteria.

This discussion has deliberately steered away from the diagnostic labels used by the American Psychiatric Association, such as attention deficit/hyperactive disorder (ADHD) (American Psychiatric Association, 1994). Developmental educators instead take the following position:

> . . . inattention, overactivity, and aggression cannot be taken as definitive evidence of ADHD. These behaviors are normal for 3- and 4-year-olds. In parent-referred problematic preschoolers, 50 percent did not exhibit significant behavior problems at age 6. Early diagnosis of ADHD can lead to misdiagnosing in significantly large numbers of young children (Tynan & Nearing, 1994), who are, therefore, labeled unnecessarily. (Hammer & Turner, 2001)

Such labeling, especially labeling a child as ADHD, should have no role in developmentally appropriate practices with children younger than ages of six or seven.

Nearly every early childhood classroom has at least one aggressive or passive child, and these children should be viewed as well within the wide category of normality. The techniques to follow should not be considered therapy. Passive, aggressive, and very difficult children are to be considered as simply stalled on a developmental railroad track. The guidance through play techniques will help the child begin once again to move down the developmental railroad track (Saltz et al., 1977) to more mature behavior.

Summary

Children from ages two to seven are moving through the four worlds of Inside Self (passivity), Body Self (physical aggression), Outside Self (verbal aggression), and Social Self (use of language and rational thinking) as they become more mature. As teachers daily perform limit setting and offer guidance of the young child, they must keep the construct of impulse control in mind. The toddler, especially in group settings, will show aggressive and passive behaviors, even if the environment is properly organized, while the three-year-old will normally respond as in our ice cream–sandbox example; however, by ages four and then five and six, the child with developmentally appropriate experiences will gain much impulse control. Helping the aggressive and passive children who at ages four, five, and later act like toddlers will be the main focus of the techniques to follow, while the same techniques may be used in dealing with toddlers.

REFERENCES

Ainsworth, M. D. S. (1995). *The development during infancy.* Dubuque, IA: Brown & Benchmark.
American Psychiatric Association. (1994). *Diagnostic and statistical manual of mental disorders* (4th ed.). Washington, DC: Author.
Atlas, J. A., & Lapidus, L. B. (1987). Patterns of symbolic expression in subgroups of childhood psychoses. *Journal of Clinical Psychology, 43,* 177–188.
Axline, V. (1969). *Play therapy* (rev. ed.). New York: Ballantine Books.
Dreikurs, R., Grunwald, B. G., & Pepper, F. C. (1989). *Maintaining sanity in the classroom: Classroom management techniques* (2nd ed.). Washington, DC: Taylor and Francis.
Erikson, E. H. (1963). *Childhood and society* (rev. ed.). New York: W. W. Norton.
Escalona, S. (1968). *The roots of individuality.* Chicago: Aldine.
Freud, A. (1974). *The ego and the mechanisms of defense.* New York: International Universities Press.
Gottman, J. M. (1977). Toward a definition of social isolation in children. *Child Development, 48,* 513–517.
Hammer, J., & Turner, P. H. (2001). *Parenting in contemporary society* (4th ed.), p. 348. Boston: Allyn and Bacon.
Ianotti, R. J. (1978). Effect of role-taking experience on role-taking, empathy, altruism, and aggression. *Developmental Psychology, 14,* 119–124.
Krown, S. (1969). *Threes and fours go to school.* Upper Saddle River, NJ: Prentice Hall.
Mahler, M. (1970). *On human symbiosis and the vicissitudes of individuation.* New York: International Universities Press.
Mahler, M., Pine, S., & Bergman, A. (1975). *The psychological birth of the human infant.* New York: Basic Books.

Peller, L. E. (1959). Libidinal phases, ego development and play. *Psychoanalytical study of the child* (p. 9). New York: International Universities Press.

Saltz, E., Dixon, D., & Johnson, J. (1977). Training disadvantaged preschoolers on various fantasy activities: Effects on cognitive functioning and impulse control. *Child Development, 48,* 367–380.

Saltz, E., & Johnson, J. (1974). Training for thematic-fantasy play in culturally disadvantaged children: Preliminary results. *Journal of Educational Psychology, 66,* 623–630.

Smilansky, S. (1968). *The effects of sociodramatic play on disadvantaged preschool children.* New York: John Wiley and Sons.

Smilansky, S., & Shefatya, L. (1990). *Facilitating play: A medium for promoting cognitive, socio-emotional and academic development in young children.* Gaithersburg, MD: Psychosocial & Educational Publications.

Spitz, R. A. (1957). *No and yes.* New York: International Universities Press.

Spitz, R. A. (1965). *The first year of life.* New York: International Universities Press.

Sroufe, L. A., & Cooper, R. G. (1999). *Child development: Its nature and course.* New York: Knopf.

Swallow, W. K. (2000). *The shy child: Helping children triumph over shyness.* New York: Warner Books.

Tynan, W., & Nearing, J. (1994). The diagnosis of attention deficit hyperactivity disorder in young children. *Infants and Young Children, 6(4),* 13–20.

Vinturella, L., & James, R. (1987). Sand play: A therapeutic medium with children. *Elementary School Guidance and Counseling, 21,* 229–238.

SUGGESTED READINGS

Adelman, H. S., and Tayler, L. (1989). *An introduction to learning disabilities.* Glenview, IL: Scott, Foresman.

Allesandri, S. M. (1991). Play and social behavior in maltreated preschoolers. *Development and Psychopathology, 3,* 191–205.

Egeland, B., & Farber, E. A. (1984). Infant-mother attachment: Factors related to its development and changes over time. *Child Development, 55,* 753–771.

Fagot, B. I., Hagan, R., Youngblade, L. M., & Potter, L. (1989). A comparison of the play behaviors of sexually abused, physically abused, and non-abused children. *Topics in Early Childhood Special Education, 9,* 88–100.

Hetherington, E. M., Cox, M., & Cox, R. (1979). Play and social interaction in children following divorce. *Journal of Social Issues, 35,* 26–49.

Hill, P., & McCune-Nicolich, L. M. (1981). Pretend play and patterns of cognition in Down's syndrome children. *Child Development, 52,* 611–617.

Horne, E. M., & Philleo, C. F. (1942). A comparative study of the spontaneous play activities of normal and mentally defective children. *Journal of Genetic Psychology, 61,* 32–36.

Joffe, L. S., & Vaughn, B. E. (1982). Infant-mother attachment: Theory, assessment, and implications for development. In B. B. Wolman (Ed.), *Handbook of Developmental Psychology* (pp. 190–207). Upper Saddle River, NJ: Prentice Hall.

Ladd, G. W., & Price, J. M. (1987). Predicting children's school adjustment following the transition from preschool to kindergarten. *Child Development, 58,* 171–178.

Siegel, L. S. (1984). Home environmental influences on cognitive development in pre-term and full-term children during the first five years." In A. W. Gottfried (Ed.), *Home environment and early cognitive development: Longitudinal research* (pp. 69–76). New York: Academic Press.

Slade, A. (1987). Quality of attachment and early symbolic play. *Developmental Psychology, 23,* 78–85.

Weiner, E. A., & Weiner, E. J. (1974). Differentiation of retarded and normal children through toy-play analysis. *Multivariate Behavior Research, 9,* 245–252.

Wing, L., Gould, J., Yeates, S. R., & Brierly, L. M. (1977). Symbolic play in severely mentally retarded and in autistic children. *Journal of Child Psychology and Psychiatry, 18,* 167–178.

Wulff, S. B. (1985). The symbolic and object play of children with autism: A review. *Journal of Autism and Development Disorders, 15,* 139–148.

C H A P T E R

2 Play and Development

In marked contrast to those nonproductive (passive or aggressive) children discussed in Chapter 1, the majority of preschoolers actively engage in mastery of the preschool classroom. These children can be described as:

1. Being high-spirited, positive, and self-assertive
2. Having some fears and initial misgivings but still ready to try new things
3. Constantly talking, making contacts with the teacher and children
4. Suggesting new ideas, relating experiences, giving instructions, and asking questions
5. Being fascinated by things around them: taking them apart and trying them out
6. Describing what they have observed, noticing differences and similarities
7. Classifying things into groups [a theoretical explanation will be given as to why classification is so important]
8. Looking for "why's" and "how's" of occurrences (causation)
9. Being full of ideas in their play with much initiative in carrying them out (Krown, 1969, p. 55)

It is within the context of play that this book will attempt to provide a program of stimulating the nonproductive child. While productive children are viewed as full of ideas for play and able to carry out ideas, the nonproductive child is unable to engage in forms of age-appropriate play.

Play: The Key to the Child's Full Development

The young child is not born with the ability to "get along" with others or to cooperate in activities of give and take. This skill of learning to live and work with others begins in the first year of life; the ability to be truly cooperative is normally accomplished by age seven, when we see children gaining the ability to play games with rules (Erikson, 1950; Freud, 1974; Herron & Sutton-Smith, 1971; Hughes, 1995; Sutton-Smith, 1980). It is in the early years that children move through pre-stages to cooperation (Burton-Jones, 1967). These pre-stages are

1. unoccupied behavior
2. solitary independent play

3. onlooker
4. parallel play
5. associative play
6. cooperative play (Parten, 1971)

Cooperative play occurs when the young child has developed the ability for socio-dramatic play (see Figure 2.1 for fuller definitions and examples of these stages).

FIGURE 2.1   Social Stages (from Parten, 1971)

Stage 1, Unoccupied Behavior: The child apparently is not playing, but occupies himself with watching anything that happens to be of momentary interest. When there is nothing exciting taking place, he plays with his own body, gets on and off chairs, just stands around, follows the teacher, or sits in one spot glancing round the room.

Stage 2, Solitary Independent Play: The child plays alone and independently with toys that are different from those used by the children within speaking distance and makes no effort to get close to other children. He pursues his own activity without reference to what others are doing.

Stage 3, Onlooker: The child spends most of his time watching the other children play. He often talks to the children whom he is observing, asks questions, or gives suggestions, but does not overtly enter into the play himself. This type differs from the unoccupied in that the onlooker is definitely observing particular groups of children rather than just anything that happens to be exciting. The child stands or sits within speaking distance of the group so that he can see and hear everything that takes place.

Stage 4, Parallel Activity: The child plays independently, but the activity he chooses naturally brings him among other children. He plays with toys that are like those the children around him are using, but he plays with the toy as he sees fit and does not try to influence or modify the activity of the children near him. He plays beside rather than with the other children. There is no attempt to control the coming or going of children in the group.

Stage 5, Associative Play: The child plays with other children. The conversation concerns the common activity; there is a borrowing and loaning of play materials; following one another with trains or wagons; mild attempts to control which children may or may not play in the group. All the members engage in similar if not identical activity; there is no division of labor and no organization of the activity of several individuals around any material goal or product. The children do not sub-ordinate their individual interests to that of the group; instead, each child acts as he wishes. By his conversation with the other children one can tell that his interest is primarily in his associations, not in activity. Occasionally, two or three children are engaged in no activity of any duration, but are merely doing whatever happens to draw the attention of any of them.

Stage 6, Cooperative or Organized Supplementary Play: The child plays in a group that is organized for the purposes of making some material product, or of striving to attain some competitive goal, or of dramatizing situations of adults and group life, or playing formal games. There is a marked sense of belonging or of not belonging to the group. The control of the group situation is in the hands of one or two of the members who direct the activity of the others. The goal as well as the method of attaining it necessitates a division of labor, taking of different roles by the various group members, and organization of activity so that the efforts of one child are supplemented by those of another.

In the prestages, unoccupied behavior is introverted and nonactive, but in solitary and independent play the child begins to manipulate objects and begins to make believe, although by himself. This is followed by parallel play (Bakeman & Brownlee, 1980; Howes, Unger, & Seidner, 1989), which can be seen when older toddlers play side by side, each doing a similar imitative activity (for example, washing dolls) but without true communication or cooperation.

The true social stage of play, near age three, is associative play, in which the children work on one task, sharing materials with peers. Two children might build a garage with blocks or work together to create a sand "city." Later, after much experience with other children, we begin to see the development of highly valued sociodramatic play as true cooperative play. This is the dress-up and make-believe role play that adults find so appealing during the preschool to kindergarten years (ages three to seven). Young children learn to understand social roles through role playing mommy, daddy, doctor, grocer, firefighter, and a host of other roles that they have seen in their culture (Connolly, 1980; Connolly, Doyle, & Ceschin, 1983; Howes et al., 1989; Howes, Unger, & Matheson, 1992a, 1992b; Rubin, 1980, 1986; Smith & Connolly, 1972).

Finally, near the beginning of middle childhood (ages seven to eleven) and the beginning of formal schooling, the child acquires the ability to play games with rules (Herron & Sutton-Smith, 1971; Piaget, 1951; Ross & Kay, 1980; Sutton-Smith & Roberts, 1970). These include competitive games (sports and board games) and mental games (word games and those often played in the car while traveling). Figure 2.2 shows the age at which most children normally acquire this social ability.

The Value of Play for Emotional Development

A young child, whose language is limited, is better able to express his feelings and understand his world through play than through complicated words. The child who has had a highly emotional negative experience (such as a trip to the dentist) or a positive experience (a birthday party) can retreat to his or her play world and play out "dentist" or "birthday." This recreation in the safe world of play allows the child to digest both pleasant and unpleasant experiences to better understand them and to begin to gain some control over his or her feelings related to the experiences. Fantasy

FIGURE 2.2   **Age Line of Social Stages**

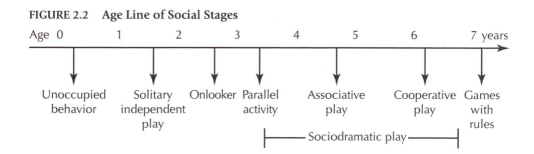

or make-believe play is a built-in therapy system for the well-developing young child (Axline, 1969; Erikson, 1950; Feshback, 1979; Ianotti, 1978; Jackowitz & Watson, 1980; Klein, 1955; Peller, 1959).

The Value of Play for Intellectual Development

Learning is not simply a process of putting information into the child and then having the child put it out. The child must play with the new information to understand it (Flavel, 1985; Piaget, 1951; Sylva, 1977; Vygotsky, 1976). Children use toys and gestures symbolically in play as attempts to understand objects and experiences in their real world (Athey, 1984; Golomb, 1979).

The symbols (Bruner, 1974; Copple, Cocking, & Mathews, 1984; Homann & Weikart, 1995; Piaget, 1951) seen in children's play and artwork indicate the development of the ability to use representation (one thing stands for another). Just as a block can symbolize (Singer, 1973) or represent a truck for the four- or five-year-old child, the letters C-A-T will represent the animal that says "meow" to the older, school-age child. The young child needs many experiences of playing with symbols before he or she is ready to unlock the world of words (the letters C-A-T stand for the animal: cat), and this is required for success in beginning reading (Bruner, 1974; Garvey, 1977). It is during the preschool years that the child is moving from the make-believe symbols (Bretherton, 1984; Bretherton & Walters, 1984; Mathews, 1977) in play to the world of words in reading and writing.

The Value of Play for Physical Development

It is through sensorimotor play (play using both the senses and muscles) that the infant or toddler discovers his or her own body and its abilities. The preschool child is still developing this awareness through both small-muscle activity (getting hands and eyes to work together) and large-muscle activity (crawling, walking, running, balancing, and climbing). It is also through play with the senses of taste, smell, touch, sight, and hearing that feelings become coordinated and useful for testing and gathering information about the world. The sensorimotor play of preschool children helps them master both understanding of their bodies and the ability to control the use of their bodies more effectively.

What Is Play?

Play, broadly defined, is an activity engaged in for the purpose of enjoyment. The play of children helps them to understand and master their feelings and to practice and master new intellectual, social, and physical skills. In order to discuss and effectively use play activities, the classroom teacher must understand the terms used to describe the various forms of play.

Sensorimotor play is the free movement of small and large muscles and the exploring of body senses to give the body practice with its sensorimotor functions. Some examples of sensorimotor play include making countless mud pies or riding endless hours on a tricycle.

In the development of sensorimotor play, the three-year-old still needs a great deal of time and space for sensorimotor practice. As the other forms of play develop (sociodramatic and construction), the preschooler seems to need to devote less time to body practice. This need continues to lessen as the child grows older. Finally, around age seven, these motor activities begin to be tied to rules and become the middle childhood (ages seven to eleven), games-with-rules type of play.

Symbolic play is make-believe play in which children express their ideas through gestures or the movement of toys or objects. Symbolic play is sociodramatic when the child

1. Undertakes a make-believe role and expresses it in imitative actions, as in pretending to be mommy, daddy, firefighter, doctor, and others
2. Uses gestures and objects to represent an imaginary object, such as a small block for daddy's electric razor
3. Persists in role play—the child stays with a single role or related roles for most of a five-minute time period or longer
4. Interacts with at least one other player within the framework of the sociodramatic play episode
5. Verbally communicates—there is some verbal interaction related to a sociodramatic play episode between two or more children

The development of symbolic play begins around age two, when we first see the toddler pretending to drink from a cup or speak on the telephone, and it makes

FIGURE 2.3 Sensorimotor Play

FIGURE 2.4 Symbolic Play

Micro toys (miniature life)
Dramatic Play

Macro toys (child size)
Sociodramatic Play

up a large part of a three-year-old's play. The child begins to express his or her ideas in symbolic make-believe play with toys and objects. For the three-year-old, symbolic play is generally seen in the form of parallel play and sometimes in simple dramatic play. A four-year-old can usually engage in sociodramatic play, which is more complex and shows a wider scope of roles as the child moves through ages four, five, and six. Finally, at school age, the child begins to give up make-believe play and incorporates make believe into what he reads and writes. The ability to play symbolically changes as the child grows intellectually during the first seven years of life (McLoyd, 1983; Nicolich, 1977).

Construction is the making of symbolic products by using materials, such as paints, paper, clay, and a wide array of similar art materials. The symbols within the product grow, develop, and become more detailed and elaborate as the child grows intellectually and gains more skills with the materials. Because of the symbols used, construction is considered a form of representational play.

The child's symbolic growth can also be evaluated through art activities, a form of construction play. If you look closely what the child produces in such construction as finger painting, easel painting, clay sculpting, and so on, you will find symbol development. As an example, look at the key symbols that develop in drawing or painting. In drawing, the child first does random scribbling, then controlled scribbling, then basic shapes, then representations of objects using basic shapes (such as a person or a house).

The human figure evolves into the face-like house, as an example, and does appear as such in many children's symbolic development. However, each child expresses the symbolic objects that are most meaningful for him, and some may not draw a human figure or a house. What is important to understand is that no matter what symbols children draw, they will progress with experience and intellectual growth through very similar development and changes. You will find it helpful to save samples of the child's products over a period of many weeks. Mark them with the date and place them in sequence so that you will have a concrete record of the child's symbolic development.

Three-dimensional materials such as clay follow a similar line of development. In working with clay, expect to see

1. Random pounding
2. Controlled pounding
3. Rolling clay into snake-like rolls and later into circles
4. Adding of pieces to the rolls and circles (facial features and body parts)
5. Combining products, such as people in cars or a boy on a horse

Development in clay as three-dimensional art could be sketched in the child's chart to keep a record of his progress in the use of that particular media, or a photograph can be taken of it with the date on the name or label that the child gives to the clay object.

Games with rules require socially agreed upon rules to hold together the co-operative play. Since most preschoolers do not yet have the intellectual ability to understand the point of view of others, they usually are unable to engage productively in games with rules that involve other participants. Only the simplest games with rules, such as Lotto, are appropriate for the preschool child.

Play and Its Development

The play of children during the preschool years will change in its complexity and duration as the child matures socially, emotionally, intellectually, and physically. The three-year-old child will have some success with construction using media such as crayons or paints but will find working with clay or three-dimensional media difficult. This will change as the child matures and gains experience and mastery over materials. Figure 2.5 should be viewed as a hypothetical representation of 100 percent of a child's developmental play capacities between ages two to seven. The figure is intended to show that the child's need for large physical practice of sensorimotor play dominates his activities at age two (Zelazo & Kearsley, 1980), but this need decreases with increasing age (Roggman, 1989) until at the age of seven this sensorimotor play becomes games with rules. Symbolic play can be seen with two-year-old children (Shimada, Sano, & Peng, 1979; Ungerer, Zelazo, Kearsley, & O'Leary, 1981) and continues throughout ages three, four, five, and six (Pederson, Rook-Green, & Elder, 1981). Near the age of seven this symbol interest changes to symbols as written words in books and reading. Finally, in contrast, although the two-year-old child will have difficulty creating recognizable symbols in construction such as painting and clay, this ability increases near age seven (hobbies of building and making objects) and on into the later years, including adulthood. The central goal of play intervention is to help the young child develop self-control and expressive abilities through the development of his symbolic abilities both in symbolic play and construction. This will lay the foundation for the ability to understand and use school skills successfully (Ladd & Price, 1987; Ladd, Price, & Hart, 1988).

Construction Materials

Fluid Materials

Play materials (Schwartzman, 1986) such as water, finger paints, dry sand (Allan & Berry, 1987; Hartley, 1971, Hartley, Frank, & Goldenson, 1952; Hartley & Goldenson, 1963; Vinturella & James, 1987), easel paints, wet sand, clay or flour and water

FIGURE 2.5   Developmental Play Capacities of the Young Child
(percentage of time, form of play, across age levels)

Age	0% 20% 40% 60% 80% 100%					
2	Sensorimotor					Symbolic
3	Sensorimotor				Symbolic	Construction
4	Sensorimotor		Symbolic			Construction
5	Sensorimotor	Symbolic			Construction	
6	Sensorimotor	Symbolic		Construction		
7	Games with rules	Symbolic (changes to reading activities)	Construction			

dough, and crayons or pens are fluid materials (see Figure 6.1). By their nature, they encourage the child to explore them through sensorimotor play. To produce symbolic construction and products, the child must control or master the materials; the child must deliberately structure the materials to his or her liking. After starting with the use of brush and paints on the paper (sensorimotor), the child next moves through the stages of symbolic development—Stage 1 (random scribbling), Stage 2 (controlled scribbling), Stage 3 (circle)—to the stages of two- and, later, three-dimensional drawing. This type of progress occurs with most of the fluids, with the exception of water and dry sand.

Structured Materials

The materials that are solid and maintain their shape and form are called structured materials. These include unit blocks (Benish, 1978; Hartley, 1971; Hartley et al., 1952; Hartley & Goldenson, 1963; Kinsman & Berk, 1979; Rogers, 1985), form boards, Legos, Montessori materials, and puzzles. They basically maintain their shape and, at the most structured form, have a minimum degree of freedom with which they should be used. Lotto games may be considered most structured because they require an adult to teach the rules and to monitor and supervise a game that would be played by a young child. Often the symbols are built in. For example, puzzles have a set form and can be used in only one way. As we move to the more open end of structured materials, the materials begin to have a less clearly defined use. The child begins to structure and change the materials to fit his own symbolic ideas. For example, blocks, the least structured of the structured materials, maintain their shape, form, and size, but the child can work with these givens and arrange the material to make any symbolic product he may wish to create. You will see symbolic growth in the use of less structured material similar to that in the fluids. Block play will first be random, then controlled, and eventually more elaborate.

Symbolic Materials

Symbolic materials both micro (small) and macro (large) encourage make-believe play. Micro symbol toys include such items as small people figures, zoo and farm animals, small playhouses and furniture, small vehicles, puppets, and other toys that are generally used in hand play. In the micro world of toys (Pulaski, 1973), the child can create elaborate make-believe dramatic episodes.

Macro symbolic toys and equipment include such items as housekeeping equipment of all kinds (stove, iron, ironing board, sink, refrigerator), costume boxes for dress-up clothing, toy luggage, toy telephones, and larger dolls. The large equipment permits the child to develop symbolic play into sociodramatic play with other children in the larger classroom space.

It pays to have on hand a well-balanced supply of materials for construction, ranging from fluid to structured, as well as abundant symbolic materials, both micro and macro (Rabinowitz, Moely, Finkel, & McClinton, 1975). Finally, the amount of

FIGURE 2.6   A Continuum of Fluid Materials (open to structured)

| Water play | Sand play | Finger painting |
| Easel painting | Clay sculpting | Drawing |

each will depend on the age level of the children. Keep in mind that the materials should parallel the amount of sensorimotor play, symbolic play, and construction play seen in Figure 2.7.

The Play Classroom

Dealing with the very difficult child requires a highly complex collection of materials, objects, and furniture arranged in a skilled manner and balanced* to support all of the major forms of play—micro symbolic (miniature toys for dramatic play), macro symbolic (dress-up items for sociodramatic play), fluid construction (water

*For a complete explanation of the methods for organizing an effective play environment or classroom, see Wolfgang & Wolfgang (2000).

FIGURE 2.7   Structured Materials

| Blocks | Legos/Interlocking shapes | Montessori equipment |
| Sorting and matching | Puzzles | Lotto games |

and sand play, paints, clay, etc.), and structured construction (blocks, Legos, puzzles, and similar manipulatives).

Consider this model layout for a play preschool classroom (see Figure 2.9). In one corner of the room near the sink and water fountain and on the section of the floor covered with linoleum are two 2-sided easels for painting, a water table, and two circular tables—one with earthen clay and shaping tools and the second containing scissors, paste, paper, and various scrap items such as aluminum foil and toilet-paper rolls for making art products. This is the fluid construction area.

Moving clockwise around the classroom, we find a large floor space sectioned off by shelving on three sides and filled with an abundant collection of unit blocks. One shelf is on wheels, which permits the teacher to swing this shelving back. Since this floor is covered with a rug, this block area now changes to the place for circle time. On the block shelves are fruit baskets with handles containing micro symbolic toys of miniature animals, people, and toy furniture that, once block construction is

FIGURE 2.8   Fluid, Structured, and Symbolic Materials

This list is provided to give examples. Many other materials could easily be added to each category.

Fluid
Water play toys; bubble set; finger painting materials; clay on wooden clay board; sand and sand toys; sand or water table with aluminum or plastic measuring cups, hand water pump, siphon, hose, funnels, sand tools, can and sifter set; unbreakable small family figures and animals; balances; boats; scoops; double easels with nonspill paint pots and smocks; felt-tip markers; colored chalk; wax crayons

Structured
Inlay puzzles; matching games; hammer, nails, and soft wood with work bench; unit blocks; giant blocks; play planks; scissors; variety of paper, paste, paper punch, felt pieces, bits of cloth, bits of wood, yarn, and pipe cleaners; typewriter; manipulative materials (string and beads, sewing basket, chunky nuts, pegboard, lacing boards); interlocking blocks; sorting boards and box for shape, color, and size; simple card games; dominos and number boards or games; stand-up mirrors

Symbolic

Micro (miniature toys): Washable, unbreakable dolls for dressing and undressing; assorted floor blocks with small family figures; farm and zoo animal sets; puppets; animal families; wooden vehicles; table blocks; open-top doll house, including furniture and people

Macro (child-size props): Housekeeping equipment of all kinds; costume box for "dress-up" clothes; toy luggage; steering wheel; ride-a-stick horse; sheet or blanket for play tent; large cartons for making stores, houses, gas stations, and for climbing into; rocking chair; large cuddly toy animals; dolls of all types; doctor equipment; plastic food; balance scales; cash register and play money; variety of hats; toy telephones

completed, can be brought out by the children for dramatic play. This is the area for structured construction play with blocks and then dramatic play with micro toys—fantasy play in the miniature world.

Moving again to the right, another zone is sectioned off for sociodramatic play, which contains child-sized furniture for both a make-believe kitchen and bedroom with supportive props of pots and pans, eating and cooking utensils, hats, scarves, adult shoes, dolls, and a host of similar materials. Stacked nearby are sturdy hinged, lidded prop boxes, each labeled with the clothing and props inside—firefighter, police officer, doctor, carpenter, and so on—to support a wide variety of roles.

Next is the structured construction area. This area is sectioned off on two sides with shelving that contains puzzles, Legos, table blocks, and various form boards. This zone is organized snugly around two small, single child-sized tables, with one table for independent construction play and one circular table where items can be placed in the middle and shared with groups of children.

FIGURE 2.9   Map of Play Classroom

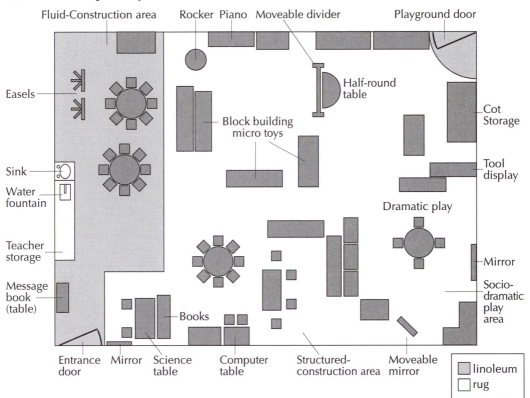

This classroom environment contains all of the basic play materials needed to support the age-appropriate play* of preschoolers, with a similar organization and arrangement on the playground to support dramatic and sociodramatic play, fluid construction, and structured construction. In an open outdoor space, large-muscle equipment is added that will help the child develop the fundamental movement patterns of walking, running, jumping, throwing, catching, and kicking (Curtis, 1982).

Summary

Characteristic of difficult children is their inability to play effectively, especially in forms of social play. This chapter has covered the social stages (unoccupied behavior, solitary independent play, onlooker, parallel play, associative play, and cooperative play), the value of play for development, and the various classifications of play

---

*Other possible materials include a fish tank, nature displays including livestock, one or two computers, space to display topical and seasonal items for children's inspection, and, of course, a book area.

(sensorimotor, symbolic, construction, and games with rules), as well as the materials (symbolic micro and macro toys and construction materials such as fluid and structured items) used in the preschool play enviornment. We are now prepared to describe a guidance program through play for passive and aggressive preschoolers.

REFERENCES

Allan, J., & Berry, P. (1987). Sandplay. *Elementary School Guidance and Counseling, 21*, 300–306.

Athey, I. (1984). Contributions of play to development. In T. D. Yawkey & A. D. Pellegrini (Eds.), *Child's play: Development and applied* (pp. 125–143). Hillsdale, NJ: Erlbaum.

Axline, V. (1969). *Play therapy* (rev. ed.). New York: Ballantine Books.

Bakeman, R., & Brownlee, J. (1980). The strategic use of parallel play: A sequential analysis. *Child Development, 51*, 873–878.

Benish, J. (1978). *Blocks: Essential equipment for young children.* Charleston: West Virginia State Department of Education. (ERIC Document Reproduction Service No. 165–901).

Burton-Jones, N. G. (1967). An ethnological study of some aspects of social behavior of children in nursery school. In D. Morris (Ed.), *Primate ethnology.* London: Weidenfeld and Nicholson.

Bretherton, I. (1984). Representing the social world in symbolic play: Reality and fantasy. In I. Bretherton (Ed.), *Symbolic play: The development of social understanding* (pp. 32–48). New York: Academic Press.

Bretherton, I., & Waters, E. (1984). The development of representation from 10 to 28 months: Differential stability of language and symbolic play. In R. Emde & R. Harmon (Eds.), *Continuities and discontinuities in development* (pp. 175–190). New York: Plenum.

Bruner, J. S. (1974). The growth of representational process in children. In J. M. Anglin (Ed.), *Beyond the information given* (pp. 313–324). New York: W. W. Norton.

Connolly, J. A. (1980). *The relationship between social pretend play and social competence in preschoolers: Correctional and experimental studies.* Unpublished doctoral dissertation, Concordia University, Irvine, CA.

Connolly, J., Doyle, A., & Ceschin, F. (1983). Forms and function of social fantasy play in preschoolers. In M. B. Less (Ed.), *Social and cognitive skills: Sex roles and children's play* (pp. 71–92). New York: Academic Press.

Copple, C. E., Cocking, R. R., & Mathews, W. S. (1984). Objects, symbols, and substitutes: the nature of the cognitive activity during symbolic play. In T. D. Yawkey & A. D. Pellegrini (Eds.), *Child's play: Development and applied* (pp. 105–124). Hillsdale, NJ: Erlbaum.

Curtis, S. M., and Brainerd, C. J., (1982). *The joy of movement in early childhood.* New York: Teachers College Press.

Day, B. (1988). *Early childhood education: Creative learning activities.* (3rd ed.). New York: Macmillan.

DeMyer, M. K., Mann, N. A., Tilton, J. R., & Loew, L. H. (1967). Toy play behavior and use of body by autistic and normal children as reported by mothers. *Psychological Reports, 21*, 975–981.

Erikson, E. (1950). *Childhood and society.* New York: W. W. Norton.

Feshback, N. D. (1979). Empathy training: A field study of affective education. In S. Feshback & A. Faazeh (Eds.), *Aggression and behavior change: Biological and social process* (pp. 15–45). New York: Praeger.

Flavel, J. H. (1985). *Cognitive development* (2nd ed.). Upper Saddle River, NJ: Prentice Hall.

Freud, A. (1974). *The ego and the mechanisms of defense.* New York: International Universities Press.

Garvey, C. (1977). *Play.* Cambridge, MA: Harvard University Press.

Golomb, C. (1979). Pretense play: A cognitive perspective. In N. Smith & M. Franklin (Eds.), *Symbolic functioning in childhood* (pp. 175–189). New York: John Wiley and Sons.

Hartley, R. E. (1971). Play: The essential ingredient. *Childhood Education*, November, 80–82.

Hartley, R. E., Frank, L. K., & Goldenson, R. M. (1952). *Understanding children's play.* New York: Columbia University Press.

Hartley, R. E., & Goldenson, R. M. (1963). *The complete book of children's play* (rev. ed.). New York: Crowell.

Herron, R. N. E., & Sutton-Smith, B. (1971). *Child's play*. New York: John Wiley and Sons.

Homann, M., & Weikart, D. (1995). *Educating young children: Active learning practices for preschool and child care programs*. Ypsilanti, MI: High/Scope.

Howes, C., & Matheson, C. C. (1992). Sequences in the development of competent play with peers: Social and social pretend play. *Developmental Psychology, 28*, 961–974.

Howes, C., Unger, O. A., & Matheson, C. C. (1992). *The collaborative construction of pretend*. Albany, NY: State University of New York Press.

Howes, C., Unger, O., & Seidner, L. B. (1989). Social pretend play in toddlers: Parallels with social play and solitary pretend. *Child Development, 60*, 77–84.

Hughes, F. P. (1995). *Children, play, and development*. Boston: Allyn and Bacon.

Ianotti, R. J. (1978). Effect of role-taking experiences on role-taking, empathy, altruism, and aggression. *Developmental Psychology, 14*, 119–124.

Jackowitz, E. R., & Watson, M. W. (1980). The development of object transformations in early pretend play. *Developmental Psychology, 16*, 543–549.

Kinsman, C. A., & Berk, L. E. (1979). Joining the block and housekeeping areas: Changes in play and social behavior. *Young Children, 35*, 66–75.

Klein, M. (1955). The psychoanalytic play technique. *American Journal of Orthopsychiatry, 55*, 223–227.

Krown, S. (1969). *Threes and fours go to school*. Upper Saddle River, NJ: Prentice Hall.

Ladd, G. W., & Price, J. M. (1987). Predicting children's social and school adjustment following the transition from preschool to kindergarten. *Child Development, 58*, 171–178.

Ladd, G. W., Price, J. M., & Hart, C. H. (1988). Predicting preschoolers' peer status from their playground behavior. *Child Development, 59*, 986–991.

Mathews, W. S. (1977). Modes of transformation in the initiation of fantasy play. *Developmental Psychology, 13*, 212–216.

McLoyd, V. C. (1983). The effects of the structure of play objects on the pretend play of low-income preschool children. *Child Development, 54*, 626–635.

Nicolich, L. (1977). Beyond sensorimotor intelligence: Assessment of symbolic maturity through analysis of pretend play. *Merrill-Palmer Quarterly, 23*, 89–99.

Parten, M. B. (1971). Social play among preschool children. In R. E. Herron & B. Sutton-Smith (Eds.), *Child's play* (pp. 160–172). New York: John Wiley and Sons.

Peller, L. E. (1959). Libidinal phases, ego development and play. In *Psychoanalytical study of the child*, No. 9, pp. 65–92. New York: International Universities Press.

Pederson, D. R., Rook-Green, A., & Elder, J. L. (1981). The role of action in the development of pretend play in young children. *Developmental Psychology, 17*, 756–759.

Piaget, J. (1951). *Play, dreams, and imitation in childhood*. New York: W. W. Norton.

Pulaski, M. A. (1973). Toys and imaginative play. In J. L. Singer (Ed.), *The child's world of make-believe* (pp. 58–73). New York: Academic Press.

Rabinowitz, F. M., Moely, B. E., Finkel, N., & McClinton, S. (1975). The effects of toy novelty and social interaction on the exploratory behavior of preschool children. *Child Development, 46*, 386–289.

Rogers, D. L. (1985). Relationships between block play and social development of children. *Early Child Development and Care, 20*, 245–261.

Roggman, L. A. (1989). *Age differences in the goals of toddler play*. Kansas City, MO: Society for Research in Child Development.

Ross, H. S., & Kay, D. A. (1980). The origins of social games. In K. H. Rubin (Ed.), *Children's play* (pp. 17–31). San Francisco: Jossey-Bass.

Rubin, K. H. (1980). Fantasy play: Its role in the development of social skills and social cognitive. In K. H. Rubin (Ed.), *Children's play* (pp. 120–129). San Francisco: Jossey-Bass.

Rubin, K. H. (1986). Play, peer interaction and social development. In A. W. Gottfried & C. C. Brown (Eds.), *Play interactions: The contribution of play materials and parental involvement to children's development* (pp. 23–54). Lexington, MA: Heath.

Schwartzman, H. B. (1986). A cross-cultural perspective on child-structured play activities and materials. In A. W. Gottfried & C. C. Brown (Eds.), *Play interactions: The contribution of play materials and parental involvement to children's development* (pp. 13–30). Lexington, MA: Heath.

Shimada, S., Sano, R., & Peng, F. C. C. (1979). A longitudinal study of symbolic play in the second year of life. The Research Institute for the Education of Exceptional Children, research bulletin. Tokyo: Gakugei University.

Singer, J. L. (Ed.). (1973). *The child's world of make-believe: Experimental studies of imaginative play.* New York: Academic Press.

Smith, P. K., & Connolly, K. J. (1972). Patterns of play and social interaction in preschool children. In N. Burton-Jones (Ed.), *Ethnological studies of child behavior* (pp. 75–89). Cambridge: Cambridge University Press.

Sutton-Smith, B. (1980). Children's play: Some sources of play theorizing. In K. H. Rubin (Ed.), *Children's play* (pp. 175–189). San Francisco: Jossey-Bass.

Sutton-Smith, B., & Roberts, J. M. (1970). The cross-cultural and psychological study of games. In G. Luschen (Ed.), *The cross-cultural analysis of games* (pp. 123–140). Champaign, IL: Stripes.

Sylva, K. (1977). Play and learning. In B. Tizard & D. Harvey (Eds.), *Biology of play* (pp. 86–92). London: Heinemann.

Ungerer, J. A., Zelazo, P. R., Kearsley, R. B., & O'Leary, K. (1981). Developmental changes in the representation of objects in symbolic play from 18 to 34 months of age. *Child Development, 52,* 186–195.

Vinturella, L., & James, R. (1987). Sand play: A therapeutic medium with children. *Elementary School Guidance and Counseling, 21,* 229–238.

Vygotsky, L. S. (1976). Play and its role in the mental development of the child. In J. Bruner, A. Jolly, & K. Sylva (Eds.), *Play: Its role in development and evolution* (pp. 97–112). New York: Basic Books.

Wolfgang, C. H., & Wolfgang, M. E. (1992). *School for young children: Developmentally appropriate practices.* Boston: Allyn and Bacon.

Zelazo, P. R., & Kearsley, R. B. (1980). The emergence of functional play in infants: Evidence for major cognitive transition. *Journal of Applied Psychology, 1,* 95–117.

SUGGESTED READINGS

Bradley, R. H. (1986). Play materials and intellectual development. In A. W. Gottfried & C. C. Brown (Eds.), *Play interactions: The contributions of play materials and parental involvement to children's development* (pp. 227–252). Lexington, MA: Heath.

Golomb, C., & Cornelius, C. B. (1977). Symbolic play and its cognitive significance. *Developmental Psychology, 13,* 246–252.

Parten, M. B. (1933). Social play among preschool children. *Journal of Abnormal and Social Psychology, 28,* 136–147.

Pellegrini, A. D. (1985). Social-cognitive aspects of children's play: The effects of age, gender, and activity centers. *Journal of Applied Developmental Psychology, 6,* 129–140.

Smilansky, S. (1968). *The effects of sociodramatic play on disadvantaged preschool children.* New York: John Wiley and Sons.

Smilansky, S., & Shefatya, L. (1990). *Facilitating play: A medium for promoting cognitive, socio-emotional and academic development in young children.* Gaithersburg, MD: Psychosocial and Educational Publications.

Sylva, K., Bruner, J. S., & Genova, P. (1976). The role of play in the problem-solving of children 3–5 years old. In J. S. Bruner, A. Jolly, & K. Sylva (Eds.), *Play: Its role in development and evolution* (pp. 220–241). New York: Basic Books.

Weikart, D. (1971). *The cognitively oriented curriculum: A framework for preschool teachers.* Washington, DC: NAEYC Publication.

Wolfgang, H. C., Mackender, B., & Wolfgang, M.E. (1981). *Growing and learning through play.* Paoli, PA: Judy/Instructo.

CHAPTER

3

Understanding Guidance Methods

Setting Limits: Skilled Teacher-Child Interaction

When a teacher facilitates, intervenes, or interacts as a form of limit setting with children, her actions have an inherent degree of power (Wolfgang, 2001) and also show the amount of freedom or autonomy (Erikson, 1950) that the teacher has granted to the child to manage his own behavior. This is especially true when dealing with aggressive, passive, and very difficult preschoolers.

To understand the concept of power and structure of teacher behaviors in the process of limit setting, consider the following incident of a teacher dealing with an aggressive child in a play classroom. The teacher uses such behaviors as looking, naming, questioning, and commanding, and then taking actions. Consider these behaviors with the degree of control that the teacher is using.

Jimmy stands before the paint easel. Using a large, thick paintbrush, he dips the end into the paint pot. Soon the brush end reappears, dripping with a large glob of paint. As a classmate walks by, Jimmy turns and sticks out the brush as if it is a sword and attempts to "stab" his peer. The peer screams and runs off, much to Jimmy's delight.

The teacher (looking) sees Jimmy's actions and physically moves towards him, positioning herself behind the easel and in direct eye contact with him. She tries to catch his eye and signal her presence to him (visual prompting). In his excitement with the paintbrush, Jimmy fails to see the teacher's signals.

TEACHER (*naming*): "Jimmy, paints can be scary and sometimes hard to control. That is fun and exciting for you, but other children are frightened by the paintbrush." Jimmy is still excited as he repeatedly dips his brush into the paint and looks for another victim.

TEACHER (*questioning*): "Where does the paint go?" The teacher waits a few seconds for a reaction from Jimmy. "Do you need my help to control the brush and paint?" Jimmy still appears to be flooded with excitement.

TEACHER (*commanding*): "Jimmy, keep the paint on the paper." The teacher states his name, makes eye contact, and places her hand lightly on Jimmy's shoulder. She tells the child what to do, not what *not* to do! Jimmy still does not comply, and he turns around to the class looking for another child to scare.

TEACHER (*follow-up preparatory command—giving choices*): "Jimmy, what you are doing shows that you have forgotten how to use the paints, and if you do that again, you will need to find a new place to play. You have a choice. Keep the paint on the paper, or find another place to play." Jimmy continues to act out.

TEACHER (*acting*): The teacher moves toward Jimmy in a controlled but nonaggressive manner, takes his arm, and physically takes the brush from him and returns it to the paint pot. She physically turns him about to face the classroom, and points to the various play centers in the classroom.

TEACHER (*commanding—including giving a choice*): "Choose and go to another area to play or you may rest in the beanbag chair." Jimmy skips over to the puzzle shelf and selects his favorite puzzle.

This incident has ended successfully with Jimmy skipping off to a new play area. However, the experienced teacher realizes that in a physical intervention such as this one, some aggressive children are more likely to strike, kick, bite, or use similar forms of aggression toward the teacher. Later, methods and constructs for dealing with raw aggression will be provided, but first it is important to understand the preceding incident to explain the structure of teacher behavior and the concept of granting children power over their own actions with the use of the Teacher Behavior Continuum (TBC) and the concept of escalation from minimum to maximum use of power (see Figure 3.1).

The Teacher Behavorial Continuum (TBC)

The goal in guiding the student during times of acting out or some other form of disruptive behavior is to grant the young child as much autonomy as possible for thinking about and rationally changing his own behavior (Erikson, 1950). In a behavioral (Alberto & Troutman, 1990) or punishment-oriented compliance classroom (Canter, 1976), the child might be reprimanded and placed in time out as a punishment for his misdeed, but in a guidance program based on developmental practices, the teacher views these incidents as valuable teachable moments (DeVries & Zan, 1994).

FIGURE 3.1   Teacher Behavioral Continuum (TBC)

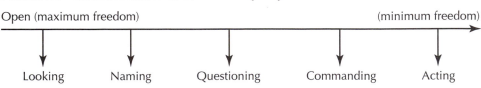

The developmental teacher wishes to grant the child full power over his own behavior, while at the same time the teacher judges the degree of safety involved and selects the degree of power of her actions to guide the out-of-control child. The TBC with its five general behaviors—looking, naming, questioning, commanding, and acting—is a construct that enables the teacher to consider the degree of power from minimum to maximum that she is using when intervening. In our example with Jimmy and the paint sword, we see the teacher first beginning with minimum power and escalating up this power continuum. Let's look at each of these TBC components to gain a full understanding of each.

Looking

> The class has just gone out to the playground. Kate has found a shovel in the sandbox and is just about to fill a bucket. Ann, seated nearby, has a bucket but no shovel. Her solution is to reach out and take Kate's shovel. Ann reaches out and takes the shovel while Kate resists, and they have a pulling match over the shovel.

> The teacher turns and looks at the two girls, but they fail to see her looking. The teacher moves to the edge of the sandbox and looks again, not breaking eye contact.

The behavior of looking, the first step on the TBC construct, involves a number of concepts: (1) the teacher's self-control (including body control), (2) proximity (proxemics), and (3) modality prompting.

Self-Control. Although the sandbox and the paint sword incidents are valuable teachable moments, they are most challenging for the teacher. The teacher is aware that in the past, when Kate was frustrated by a classmate, she lashed out violently and did some harm to other children, which produced parental complaints. The teacher, of course, feels the urgency to keep the children safe.

While looking at the sandbox incident and considering what action to take, the teacher becomes understandably tense and nervous. Let's look at a more dramatic incident to demonstrate this point. Angela, a three-year-old, has broken away from her mother's hand and has just run into a busy street, or pushed over the white-hot charcoal grill, or acted in some way that could clearly be life-threatening for her and others. Moments later, the mother is nose to nose with the child, screaming at the child never to do that again. For all intents and purposes, the mother—understandably—is hysterical and out of control, and Angela will be lucky to avoid being shaken harshly or hit. Teachers in schools and classrooms will feel similar fears and anger, but they must learn to maintain control as they deal with such dynamic incidents.

When a teacher sees these frightening, aggressive clashes between child and child or child and teacher, the teacher's fear produces a physiological response that Jones (1987, 2001) would call an *adrenaline dump*, causing a reflex body action triggered by the sight of this aggression—it evokes a type of flight-or-fight response by the teacher. The teacher is out of control as long as she in this hyperalert state, meaning that for a short period, she has lost the ability to reason and is functioning as an automatic, defensive being. Rational thinking is too slow for sudden emergencies, and the body has a built-in survival process that shuts down higher-order thinking so the defensive reflexes can act. Because of the need to keep children safe in the classroom, the aggressive actions by children will cause adrenaline dumps in teachers.

Jones (1987, 2001) describes the theory that humans have a triune brain, or three brains in one. This triune brain contains a reptilian brain located at the base of the brain stem (when we touch something hot, this brain causes us to pull our hand away immediately), a paleocortex (an ancient cortex, or "doggie-horsy" brain, which functions much like that of lower-level animals), and a neocortex (a new cortex where abstract thinking and problem solving occur). The triune brain theory suggests that each of these three brains has its own functions, and that under stress, the brain downshifts to lower primal centers for purposes of survival. Under moderate arousal, the management of behavior shifts from the neocortex to the paleocortex. Under extreme arousal, the management of behavior shifts from the paleocortex to the reptilian brain. This means that when we are angry, frightened, and very upset, we may become paleocortical, animal-like beings, and higher thinking is unavailable until we calm down.

This downshift occurs in two forms: an adrenaline dump (Jones, 1987, 2001) that can be triggered by seeing a sudden, violent action by an aggressive child, or a slow bleeding (Jones, 1987, 2001) of adrenaline into our body system, maintaining us in a constant alert and defensive, stressful state in anticipation of a potential aggressive act. The teacher experiencing a slow bleeding feels, "I must keep my eye on Jimmy every moment or he will hurt someone!"

The teacher turns to find Jimmy again at the paint easel, and the paint from all four paint pots has been spilled on the floor. He is "skating" in large pools of red, blue, yellow, and green. This is the fifth time he has done such actions this morning; the teacher feels the blood rushing to her face, her hands become clammy, she stops breathing, and her body tenses up—she has just had an adrenaline dump.

> **TEACHER** (*in a harsh voice one step short of actually shouting*)**:** "I have told you that you may not use the paints, young man! This is the fifth time that I have had to deal with you this morning, and I am sick and tired of it, do you hear! Look what you have done!" The teacher stands with her left hand on her left hip, balancing on one leg and tapping the toe of her right foot, as she points and shakes her index finger at Jimmy. "Now, you go to the time-out chair and stay there and do not get up. Do you hear what I said? Do not get up until I tell you to!" This is the "doggie-horsy" brain speaking.

This teacher is out of control. Her rational brain is no longer available to her because of her anger, and she has "downshifted" (Bailey, 2000) to the "doggie-horsy" brain as she "snaps and snarls" at Jimmy (Jones, 1987, 2001). Using the impulse control construct described in the first chapter (see Figure 1.2), the teacher is regressing from the use of language and rational thinking to that of verbal aggression. The language used when the teacher loses control is threatening, hostile, and punishing. When some aggressive children see such behavior from adults, they know intuitively that they have pushed the teacher's button. They now feel powerful and entertained that they can control the teacher's actions. As the angry teacher physically takes the child to the time-out chair, a smile of recognition (Dreikurs, 1972) appears on the child's face. He seems to enjoy the teacher's reactions, which doubly angers that teacher because the time out does not seem to be punishing enough to teach the child a lesson.

How can the teacher maintain self-control when dealing with such aggressive and destructive incidents? Looking, in the TBC construct, means that the first thing the teacher does when faced with a conflict is to stop and do nothing until she gets self-control. Responding to these incidents while angry will probably lead the teacher to take actions that are punishing, hostile, and threatening. They most likely will not work and may possibly make things worse. The first action under looking is to control physical reflex actions—posture, breathing, and eye contact. The tendency in a confrontation in the fight-or-flight stance is to body-telegraph anger (shaking one finger at the student with a hostile facial expression) or fear (turning away and dropping eye contact).

Bailey (2000) has created a mnemonic device as a way of recalling the actions the teacher must first take in the looking process—S-T-A-R:

S = Smile
T = Take a deep breath (inhale)
A = And
R = Relax (exhale)

In a tense situation, reflex behavior with its accompanying adrenaline dump causes us to tense up, regress to the "doggie-horsy" brain, and stop breathing in anticipation of fight of flight. A first step with Jimmy with the paint sword or skating in the spilled paint, or Kate and Ann fighting over a shovel in the sandbox, requires the teacher to take no verbal or physical action until she gains self-control through STAR—smile, take a deep breath (inhale), and relax (exhale). The deliberate smile takes away the angry or hostile look on the teacher's face, and the breathing relaxes the whole body. This gives her time to shift back to higher-order thinking and effective action in dealing with these situations.

Body Control.   In controlling our body while in a confrontation, we move into one of two stances: squaring off (Jones, 1987, 2001) or the supportive-defensive stance (CPI, 1987). Again, in confrontation we are unaware that we are nonverbally telegraphing (Jones, 1987, 2001) our nervous internal state. We drop our eyes, turn our body sideways as if to flee, our hands shake, and our face shows a harsh tenseness. This communicates fear or anger.

This control of one's body and the use of physical stances can be seen even between two adults in potential conflict. A father takes his teenage daughter, who has been wearing glasses for only one month, back to the optometrist to have a screw replaced on the glasses, which came out without any misuse. The receptionist turns to the daughter and asks, "How did this happen?" The daughter replies that she did not know, which is true. The receptionist then harshly reprimands her about how she must have mistreated the glasses. The harsh, unnecessary criticism causes an adrenaline dump in the father, as he feels the need to defend his daughter who had been wearing and caring for the new glasses with much pride. This produces a physical fight-or-flight response. (Daddy bear must protect baby bear). Both father and daughter first drop their heads, feeling guilty and just wanting to leave—flight. Then the father, in order to control his emotions and behavior, STARs (Bailey, 2000). He smiles, takes a deep breath (inhales), and relaxes (exhales). Then he takes a body stance of "squaring off": He stands, broadens his physical stance, places his nervous hands slightly behind his back, and makes eye contact. He then STARs for a second time to become able to speak in a reasonable and controlled manner to the accusing receptionist. "Please stop, and look at me," he says, "I need to give you some information that you do not have. This is Martha's first pair of glasses, and she has worn them proudly and has taken great care of them. You can see by her behavior that she is very saddened by your words!" He then apologizes to the receptionist and acknowledges that possibly she is just having a very bad day.

Squaring Off.   The squaring-off stance is placing one's body directly in front of the person being confronted, taking a wider and broader stance with the feet for balance, placing the hands slightly behind the back (because the hands vibrate, immediately showing nervousness), and then making unbroken eye contact (Jones, 1987, 2001). This communicates a power stance and signals "I mean business." When done while lowering the voice, the squaring-off stance gets the full attention of the person with whom we are attempting to communicate—an aggressive adult or violent child. This is not done in a hostile manner: remember, STAR.

Supportive-Defensive Stance.   The supportive-defensive (CPI, 1987) stance is different from the squaring-off stance. Squaring off outside the kicking distance of a potentially assaultive child is effective, but getting close to the angry child in a squared-off stance presents the child with the most vulnerable parts of the body (nose, throat, and groin). In a group of 300 preschool teachers, the question was asked, "Who in this group has been bitten, kicked, and struck by a preschool child?" On each question 69–89 percent of the teachers raised their hands.

To maintain physical safety when close to the child, the feet are posed in an "L" shape, presenting the side of the body toward the potentially assaultive child. Place the hands out in front and toward the child, with the palms open and down, moving the hands slowly up and down in an attempt to calm the child who is losing control. The potentially assaultive child in the fight-or-flight condition sees that there are no objects in the hands that might hurt him. If the child tries to kick or bite, our feet are in a position to permit quick movement, and any strikes on the side can do limited damage. This side stance has to be supportive of the child, attempting to get him calmed down while at the same time providing a defensive stance to deal with any real acting-out behavior.

Proxemics.   Using the general behaviors on the TBC of naming, questioning, or commanding with a young child from across the room will have minimum power and effect. If the teacher moves physically closer to that misbehaving student while maintaining eye contact and stopping approximately three feet from the child, she has increased her power-proxemics. Finally, if she takes these same actions face to face with the child six inches away, the power of naming, questioning, and commanding is dramatically increased (CPI, 1987; Jones, 1987, 2001). All people, including young children, have a privacy space of three feet. When other people, especially strangers, invade this space it naturally heightens emotional tension. When others invade our personal space, it is for the reasons of affection or aggression—people are either going to hug and kiss us or hurt us. Both conditions trigger strong emotions (Jones, 1987, 2001). To communicate with young children, especially aggressive and passive children, teachers must be aware of three levels of proxemics (Wolfgang & Wolfgang, 1995; Wolfgang, 1996): far (across the room), near (three feet), and intimate (six inches).

> TEACHER (*STARs*): "Jimmy, where does the paint go?" The teacher waits a few seconds for a reaction from Jimmy. "Do you need my help to control the brush and paint?" The teacher broadcasts this statement from across the room. Jimmy still appears to be flooded with excitement and continues his paint sword activity. Attempting to maintain eye contact with Jimmy, the teacher crosses the classroom, closing space (Jones, 1987, 2001), and stops in front of Jimmy at the three-foot range. Her posture is one of squaring off.

> TEACHER (*questioning*): "Jimmy, where does the paint go?" The teacher repeats the question like a broken record (Alberti & Emmons, 1975) in the new proxemics position of "near." "Do you need my help to control the brush and paint?" Jimmy does not acknowledge hearing the teacher because of his internal excitement. The teacher takes each of Jimmy's hands, one containing the paintbrush, in each of her hands. She then positions herself face to face with him at a six-inch range and makes unbroken eye contact, taking a supportive-defensive stance.

> TEACHER (*questioning, in a whispering soft voice*): "Jimmy, where does the paint go?" Again, the teacher continues to repeat the question, like a broken record (Alberti & Emmons, 1975) in the new proxemics position of intimate (Wolfgang & Wolfgang, 1995). "Do you need my help to control the brush and paint?"

In this example, the teacher STARs, closes space, uses proxemics (far, near, and intimate) to increase her power, changes her stance from squared-off to a supportive-defensive stance, and questions Jimmy. Proxemics and maintaining unbroken eye contact increase the power and control the structure of the teacher's actions. Confrontation through proxemics should *not* be done in an aggressive, angry manner. The teacher attempts to wash out the expression on her face so that it is flat and expressionless, or she smiles. She does not communicate approval or disapproval, but rather an attitude of "I mean business and wish you to join me in problem solving this situation." Teachers who cannot use proxemics or control their expressions body-telegraph (Jones, 1987, 2001) either hostility and anger or helplessness and fear. Notice that these are fight-or-flight responses. The skilled teacher can maintain a nonhostile position with STAR, eye contact (modality prompting), closing space when necessary, proxemics, and a squared-off or supportive-defensive stance with the aggressive child. If necessary, she can verbally respond with naming, questioning, or commanding.

Modality Prompting.   Besides using the privacy space concept, there is a second justification for proxemics. Chapter 1 describes both the passive and aggressive child as having punished modalities (Wolfgang & Wolfgang, 1995), such as hypersensitivity to touch, hearing, and seeing. We often hear adults say to children, "I have told you this a hundred times, and you're still doing this. Can't you hear me?" The answer might be no for the hypersensitive child. Maybe the child doesn't hear when in a confrontational situation. Communication with a child, especially at the intimate level, is done in nearly all modalities—touch (holding his hands), seeing (eye contact), and hearing (verbal statements). The emotionally flooded child is more likely to respond to communication in close proxemics with multiple modalities. As an aside, in group settings such as day care or preschool classrooms, the younger the child, the closer the proxemics will need to be when attempting to communicate. A toddler often will need to be communicated with at proxemics-intimate level.

Naming

If the use of prompting by looking is unsuccessful, the teacher can escalate her power by moving up the TBC to naming. If the teacher simply used looking (with proxemics and stances) in the incident with Kate and Ann fighting over the sand shovel, and if the children felt and recognized her presence and then resolved the incident themselves, the teacher has granted them much autonomy. She has expended much less energy and time in getting a potentially aggressive or assaultive incident resolved. If looking does not resolve the situation, she escalates to naming, using words or verbal communication, with verbal encoding, to describe or name the situation and/or the feelings of the child as the teacher sees them.

Verbal encoding is a very soft, noncontrolling technique. It has the sole purpose of bringing to the child a conscious awareness of his actions, his and others' feelings, and his effect on others.

Reconsider Jimmy and the paintbrush example:

> **TEACHER** (*naming/verbal encoding*): "Jimmy, paints can be scary and sometimes hard to control. That is fun and exciting for you, but other children are frightened by the paintbrush."

Chapter 1 described aggressive, passive, and very difficult preschoolers as lacking the social skills to work with others. They do not feel that they can get their needs met or depend on adults to help them meet their needs. As a result, they respond nonproductively to conflict or similar changes with passivity, physical aggression, or verbal aggression, which are fight-or-flight behaviors. The difficult child needs to reattach to a caring adult and establish a nonjudgmental relationship (Gordon, 1974, 1988) with an adult—the teacher. Difficult children who feel unloved and unaccepted must find a teacher who will value and invest in them emotionally—"love begins with love." Through first reestablishing this relationship with a dependable adult, children will regain confidence and then gradually learn to be independent and trust in themselves. The dynamic that helps develop this loving trust is the process of communication. This communication occurs when a child expresses himself verbally ("I hate this school!") or nonverbally as acting-out behavior (the child watches as other children build with blocks and then walks in and knocks them down, much to the distress of the other children). We attempt to understand what he is feeling and the difficulties that he is facing.

CHILD: "I hate this school!"

TEACHER (*naming*): "School is making you very unhappy right now."

The child knocks down the blocks of two boys whom he has been watching build and play together (acting out).

TEACHER (*naming*): "You wanted to play with the boys but did not know how. And you became angry and knocked down their blocks."

Naming, which is also called active listening (Gordon, 1974), permits the teacher to verbally label the child's first early attempts to label his needs. Relationships between both the difficult child and the teacher or even between two adults develop when the supportive adult is willing to listen nonjudgmentally to the communication of the person in need and attempts to understand the other person's feelings and problems. The child attempting to communicate, especially when he is verbally aggressive or even acting out, begins to trust the adult who does not respond with punishment but shows acceptance through active listening (Gordon, 1974, 1988) or naming. Gradually the child begins to realize that the teacher is accepting him, even when he behaves badly. This leads to a reattachment to the caring teacher.

Child Guidance Through Play values are clearly defined by Bailey (2000) as a developmentally appropriate view of young children's behavior and needs:

- It's okay to feel what you feel. Feelings are not right or wrong; they simply are. There is no one who can tell you what you should feel.
- It's good and necessary to talk about feelings.
- It's okay to ask for what you want.
- Your perceptions are valid.
- It's okay and necessary to have lots of fun and play.
- It's important to know your limits and to be able to delay gratification.
- It's crucial to develop a balanced sense of responsibility. This means accepting the consequences for what you do.
- It's okay to have problems. They need to be solved.
- It's okay to have conflict, both within yourself and with others. It needs to be resolved. (Bradshaw, 1990; Bailey, 2000)

Active listening, or naming, is a technique for improving communication between child and teacher. The child is encouraged to "talk out" repetitively, and the teacher's role is to attempt to mirror back to the child the feelings and problems she thinks she is hearing from the child. Taking first or surface communication statements from the child as fact, especially when the child is emotionally flooded, the teacher may not hear what the child is really attempting to communicate. The teacher's nonverbal behavior, such as nodding her head (called acknowledgments) (Gordon, 1974, 1988) and asking questions such as, "Would you like to tell me more?" are called door openers (Gordon, 1974, 1988). Such behavior serves to encourage the child to continue to talk and attempt to communicate.

Consider another teacher-child example:

TEACHER (*naming*): "Jimmy, paints can be scary and sometimes hard to control. That is fun and exciting for you, but other children are frightened by the paintbrush."

JIMMY: "I don't like him!" meaning another child, Walter, who just passed by and was the target of Jimmy's latest attempts to stab with the paintbrush.

TEACHER (*active listening or naming*): "You're angry with Walter?"

JIMMY: "He is mean!"

TEACHER (*active listening or naming*): "Walter has been mean to you?"

Jimmy stops talking and seems to withdraw into himself. The teacher makes eye contact, nods, and smiles (acknowledgments).

TEACHER: "Would you like to tell me more about what you are feeling?" (door opener)

JIMMY: "Yes, I am his best friend, and he let Robert sit next to him at snack!"

TEACHER (*active listening or naming*): "You're angry because you were not able to sit by your friend."

JIMMY: "Yes. Could I sit by Walter?"

The teacher's efforts to determine the cause of Jimmy's sword play have exposed a deeper problem that Jimmy is facing, and she can begin dealing with it from a new perspective.

"I"-message.   An "I"-message (Gordon, 1974, 1988) is another teacher behavior under the general category of naming on the TBC. The "I"-message is the least guilt-inducing method of directly expressing to the child how his actions are affecting the teacher and his peers. Here is an example of an "I"-message:

TEACHER: "When friends are stabbed with a wet paintbrush (behavior), it soils their clothing and scares other children (effect). I need to keep people safe and clean, and it frightens me (feeling) when people are jabbed."

The "I"-message is a way to inform the child of the problem that *you*, the teacher, are facing. The "I"-message is not saying, "You did something wrong" (the word "you" is not permitted in an "I"-message), and it is *not* saying, "Here is how I want you to change." It is *permitting* the other person to understand how you are feeling.

Generally, after the teacher delivers an "I"-message, the child might respond in one of three ways. First, he might simply stop the misbehavior (Jimmy stops the sword play and returns to painting a picture on the paper at the easel), thereby ending the teachable moment. Second, the child might continue to defy the teacher, prompting an escalation of power along the TBC to the questioning stage. Finally, the child might respond with some form of language. This language is typically of two types, either defensive language (verbal aggression, denial, or attempting to distract the teacher to a side issue) (Jones, 1987, 2001) or real verbal communication (how the child may wish to solve a specific dilemma he is facing).

Here is an example of defensive language as forms of verbal aggression and sidetracking:

> **TEACHER:** "When friends are stabbed with a wet paintbrush (behavior), it soils their clothing and scares other children (effect). I need to keep people safe and clean, and it frightens me (feeling) when people are jabbed."
>
> **JIMMY:** "I didn't do anything!" (denial) The teacher simply looks on— acknowledgment. "You're a butthead! (verbal aggression) Carol was playing sword and you didn't say anything to her!"(sidetracking)

Jimmy's response is simply an immature child's attempt to find some defensive way of handling this situation. His denial should not be viewed as lying; the teacher should simply ignore these denials as a natural tendency to deny reality as the child is faced with it. In addition, some children emotionally flood and are quite frightened; they actually may not remember what they did, even though it occurred just seconds before.

The teacher also must not be frightened, angered, or offended by "you're a butthead" (or sexual or swear words) because, according to the passive-aggressive construct as explained in Chapter 1 (see Figure 1.1), verbal aggression is a more productive response than physical aggression. The teacher must respond with "I"-messages and an attempt to understand the feelings behind the verbal aggression.

> **TEACHER:** "When those words are said to me, I hear anger, but I don't know why you're angry, and I feel sad that I am not able to help you. ("I"-message) What words could you use to help me understand what you want?" (door opener)

NOTE: The statement often used by teachers thinking they are using an "I"-message, "I don't like it when so-and-so happens!" is not an "I"-message. It is an expression of the teacher's value judgment and communicates guilt to the child.

The teacher must not be drawn into a power play (Jones, 1987, 2001) by the child's defensive attempts to make her feel guilty ("Carol was playing sword, and you didn't say anything to her!") and respond by trying to deny the child's criticism or explain her behavior to him. It has been said that the best defense at times is a good offense, so the teacher should just see this as an attempt—a fairly sophisticated one—to sidetrack her as a means to take the focus off the child and his actions. The teacher may simply ignore the statement or use some of the following techniques to respond to denial, verbal aggression, or guilt statements used by children to sidetrack.

The philosophical orientation of these relationship-listening techniques views the child as an inherently good and rational being. If the child's behavior is destructive, the relationship-listening explanation is that the child is having some form of inner turmoil, called flooding, and this inner tension comes out as acting-out behavior or verbal aggression. Thus, under *Child Guidance Through Play* philosophy, the child should never be viewed simply as being naughty. The teacher's helping role is to establish a nonjudgmental, supportive relationship with the child and to encourage the child to communicate these feelings in words, by using the teacher as a sounding board.

Here is a mother first responding with poor communication, and then with the techniques under naming to establish an accepting relationship with her daughter:

> CHILD: "Mom, when is dad going to get home from work?"
>
> MOTHER: "Ann, you know that dad always gets home at six o'clock."

The child has failed to communicate her real need, and the mother has failed to hear what was really being said. What the child really meant to say was, "Mom, I am very hungry, and I don't think I can wait until dad gets home to eat."

When the child has an inner need, she must express it externally, and so she tries verbally labeling that need to express her wants. Now, let's replay the discussion, this time with the mother using active listening (naming):

> CHILD: "Mom, when is dad going to get home from work?"
>
> MOTHER: "At six o'clock, but you would like dad to get home sooner?" (active listening)
>
> CHILD: "Ah, he'll be late again!"
>
> MOTHER: "You are worried that he might not be on time today." (active listening)
>
> CHILD: "I don't think I can wait for dad if he's going to be late."
>
> Mother looks at child, nods, and smiles—acknowledgment.
>
> CHILD: "I'm starving!"
>
> MOTHER: "You are very hungry, and you'd like to eat now and not wait for daddy because he might be late?" (active listening)
>
> CHILD: "Yeah. A-a-ah . . ."
>
> MOTHER: "You would like to tell me more?" (door opener)
>
> CHILD: "Yeah, while I was waiting for the bus it rained and I forgot to bring my lunch into the shelter. It got wet and was ruined, and all I had to eat for lunch was a banana."

MOTHER: "Oh, that does make a difference. The rule is that we wait for dad so we can all eat dinner together, but since you missed out on lunch today, why don't you have a glass of milk and two oatmeal cookies for now."

Questioning

As a classmate walks by, Jimmy turns and sticks out the brush as if it were a sword, attempting to "stab" his peer. The peer screams and runs off, much to Jimmy's delight.

The teacher sees Jimmy's actions (looking) and physically moves toward him, positioning herself behind the easel and in direct eye contact with him. She tries to catch his eye and signal him (visual prompting) to her presence. In his excitement (emotional flooding), Jimmy fails to see the teacher's signals.

TEACHER (*naming*): "Jimmy, paints can be scary and sometime hard to control. That is fun and exciting for you, but other children are frightened by the paintbrush." Jimmy is still excited as he repeatedly dips his brush into the paint and looks for another victim.

TEACHER (*questioning*): "Where does the paint go?" The teacher waits a few seconds for a reaction from Jimmy. "Do you need my help to control the brush and paint?" Jimmy still appears to be flooded with excitement.

The movement up the TBC to confronting the misbehaving child with questioning is to have the child mentally reflect on his current, past, or future behavior and come up with an idea of how to live within the rules. The teacher does not solve the problem for the child but expects him to come up with an acceptable solution himself. The question used in this step challenges the child to work through difficulties rationally and decide on more productive behavior.

Questioning While Misbehavior Is Occurring.   When moving into the dynamic interactions among the difficult child and his peers or the equipment and materials (paints and the paintbrush "sword"), the teacher should phrase her questions to permit the child to reflect and come up with a more acceptable action. "Where do the paints go?" (The teacher wants a motor action.) "What could you say to Jane when she takes your sand shovel?" (The teacher wants the child to use language.) And, then, finally, the teacher makes an offer of physical help: "Do you need my help to control the paints and paintbrush?" The teacher's questions are leading; she does not really want the child to answer her directly with language, but to act in new ways through motor actions. However, the question offering help is a serious one because some children when excited cannot physically stop themselves. They really need an adult to take their hands and move the brush back to the paper, or put the brush in the paint pot, or simply place hands on the child's back, lending them a physical presence so they can control themselves.

Questioning After the Misbehavior Has Occurred.   The use of questioning after an incident of misbehavior is confined to these four steps:

1. "Stop!"
2. "What" questions: "What did you do?" "What is the rule?"
3. Contracting: "How will you change?"
4. Relax chair (if needed).

> As a peer walks by, Jimmy turns and strikes out with the wet paintbrush, making a slashing yellow mark down his shirt.

> > TEACHER: "Stop! What did you do, Jimmy?" (Step 1)

> > JIMMY: "Wha-at?" (He is now aware that the teacher is present and is aware of his actions.)

> > TEACHER: "What did you do?" (Step 2)

> > JIMMY: "I didn't do anything! (denial) Carol was playing sword, and you didn't say anything to her!" (sidetracking)

> > TEACHER: "What did *you* do, Jimmy?" (Step 2)

> > JIMMY: "You're a butthead! (verbal aggression) Let me alone! No-o-o!" Jimmy becomes upset, puts the brush back into the paint pot, and runs off to the block corner, attempting to hide.

> The teacher goes to Jimmy, takes one of his hands in hers, and brings him back to the easel. "Jimmy, we need to talk about this. What did you do?" (Step 2)

> Jimmy drops to the floor, kicking into the air, and throwing a minor temper tantrum.

> The teacher picks up Jimmy and gently places him in a large overstuffed chair nearby. "Jimmy, this is a safe place for you to be. I want you to relax here. When you are ready to talk, I will come back and talk to you about the painting." (Step 4)

> Jimmy slouches down into the chair, drops his eyes, pouts for a period of four to six minutes, and then begins to sit up in the chair, watching other children.

> > TEACHER (*approaching Jimmy*): "I need to talk to you about the painting. What did you do?" (Step 2)

> > JIMMY: "I don't know." (or "I painted people!")

> > TEACHER: "Well, I saw what you did, and you were using the paintbrush to paint Mark. What is the rule about how paints are to be used?" (Step 2: "what" question requesting a verbal statement of the rule)

> > JIMMY (*eyes drop*): "Aah, keep the paint—ah—paper."

> > TEACHER: "Yes, when paints are used, our rule is to keep paint on the paper." The teacher restates the rule so it is very clear. "Now you and I must work this out. We must have an agreement." (Step 3) The teacher moves to Jimmy, takes him gently by the hands, and makes eye contact. "What will you do to

change? When you use the paints, again, how will you use them?" (Step 2: "what" question requesting change)

JIMMY: "Keep the paint on the paper."

TEACHER: "Yes. Do we have an agreement on this? Can I depend on you remembering the rule?" (Step 3)

JIMMY: "Yes." He looks up and makes eye contact with the teacher.

TEACHER: "Good, we now have an agreement. If you agree, I want to shake hands to show a special agreement between us." The teacher holds out her hand to Jimmy and smiles warmly. (Step 3)

Jimmy returns the teacher's smile and shakes the teacher's hand.

TEACHER: "Good, we now have an agreement! If you can now remember the painting rules, you may paint. But if you forget the rules, your behavior will say that you do not know how to use paints and you will not be able to use the easel. (Step 3: consequence) Now, you may feel free to come back to work and play with us, when you feel that you are ready."

Jimmy hops up, takes off the paint smock, hangs it on the appropriate hook, moves over to the puzzle shelf, and selects a puzzle.

Notice at the beginning of the example that the teacher did not tell the child what *not* to do, but simply stated, "Stop." The "what" questions that followed related only to what the child did, to the rule, and to a challenge for the child to come up with his own ideas of how to change.

Because of young children's irreversibility of thinking (Piaget, 1971a, 1971b), the child does not necessarily mentally reflect on his entire sequence of behavior. The child simply knows the teacher is confronting him and most likely his mind is racing through thoughts of, "Will the teacher punish me?" or, "How can I get out of this situation and away from the teacher?" The "what" question asks the child to be mentally reflective (Glasser, 1975, 1986). If the child cannot remember what happened—and some will not or cannot say it—the teacher will tell the child what did occur; however, the preference is to have the child verbally state his own actions.

The teacher does not stop the confronting process when the child responds by crying or throwing a temper tantrum because young children have discovered that such strong expressions of emotion can be a powerful technique to get the adult off their backs. The teacher responds to this emotional flooding by taking the child to a "relax chair" (Glasser, 1975, 1986; Wolfgang & Wolfgang, 1995) or an isolated space and separating the child from others for the sole purpose of permitting the child to calm down and get relaxed. The teacher reassures the child that this is a safe space and that no one will bother him or hurt him in any manner. This is not a punishment (Glasser, 1975, 1986; Dreikurs, 1964, 1968, 1972) and not a time-out (Alberto & Troutman, 1990) because, when the child is ready to contract and rationally discuss the incident, he is free to return. The teacher's voice inflection and nonverbal expressions are not ones of guilt, but take a rather matter-of-fact problem solving attitude toward the child. The teacher is not sidetracked by the child's claims of unfairness or denial or by another emotional outburst or crying (sometimes humorously called water power) (Dreikurs, 1964). Instead, the teacher remains focused on the child's behavior in this particular incident, attempting to limit any implication of guilt. The teacher's attitude toward the child is, "Look, this is not appropriate behavior here. We are faced with a problem, and I want to work with you to understand the problem and your behavior. I want to give you the power to change. I want you to commit yourself to this change through a contract or agreement."

After a contract is established between teacher and child, the child is to return to the classroom with a clean slate, meaning that the teacher must maintain an attitude of optimism. The teacher must believe—and show by her actions that she believes—that Jimmy can and will change his behavior. If she is angry at Jimmy because of his actions and she communicates this anger nonverbally, Jimmy and his classmates will sense this and he most likely will live up to her lack of faith in his ability to change—the power of expectations.

Commanding

The next teacher behavior on the TBC is giving a command. At this point in limit setting, the teacher now takes very controlling action. The teacher must state the actions she wants through the command. A command (Canter, 1976; Canter & Canter, 1992) contains the following actions by the teacher:

1. Moves to the child, kneels down to make direct eye contact
2. States the child's name
3. Gestures
4. Touches the child
5. Verbally demands that the child stop (demands a desist)
6. Demands a motor action for positive behavior by the child (tells the child what to do rather than what not to do)
7. Promises a follow-through consequence (Canter, 1976; Canter & Canter, 1992)

Note that nearly all modalities are used to communicate with this child in a command: visual, auditory, and tactile.

Consider again the example with Jimmy and see the teacher using the command.

As Robert walks by, Jimmy turns and sticks out the brush as if it were a sword and attempts to "stab" his schoolmate.

> **TEACHER** (*making eye contact*): "Jimmy (states his name in a nonthreatening but firm voice), stop." She verbally demands a desist and gestures by pointing to the brush and then the paper and touches the child by placing her right hand on Jimmy's left shoulder. "Use the brush to paint on the paper." She demands a positive behavior action. "The rule is that we do not hit others. If you cannot follow the rule, I will take you out of the painting area and ask you to go to another area." She promises a follow-through consequence.
>
> **JIMMY:** "But Robert won't be my friend!"

TEACHER: "Use the brush to paint on the paper. The rule is that we do not hit others."

JIMMY: "No, this is my brush!"

TEACHER: "Use the brush to paint on the paper. The rule is that we do not hit others." (broken record)

JIMMY: "No, I am going to hit you! You butthead!"

TEACHER: "Use the brush to paint on the paper. The rule is that we do not hit others." (broken record)

Developmentally Appropriate View.   When a child acts in an inappropriate manner in the classroom, the beginning teacher may ask, "What should be done to stop this behavior?" The natural tendency, especially for a beginning or unskilled teacher, is to rush toward the child, state in a loud and forceful manner (high-profile desist) (Kounin, 1977) what the child must *not* do ("Don't do that, Walter. Stop clowning around!"), and then, if compliance is not obtained, physically remove the child. This approach of telling the child what *not* to do instead of giving the child a command is generally ineffective for a number of reasons.

Erikson (1950) characterizes the preschool-age years as the period when the child appears to be emotionally pulled between the two extremes of initiative and guilt. These preschoolers want to initiate creative ideas and actions (Jimmy's sword painting) but as yet cannot narrow their behavior into socially acceptable rules and limits. Thus, when they break rules, they are overwhelmed by feelings of guilt (Erikson, 1950). When placed in this spotlight, after some incidents of rule breaking or misbehavior, they are emotionally flooded with feelings of shame and guilt. At the preschool age, feelings of guilt are deeply felt emotions fully ready to effervesce and can be quickly triggered by adult demands. "Don't do it!" brings quick and strong defensive emotional feelings from the child at this particular age and is highly likely to flood the child with emotion. This flooding clouds the preschool-age child's logical thinking on how to respond to the teacher's demand. Thus, the "don't do" statements are likely to cause feelings of guilt or inferiority or make the child confused and respond in an aggressive or foolish and destructive manner toward the teacher.

In viewing the command component of the TBC, keep in mind the way in which young children hear and absorb verbal communication when they are emotionally flooded. When emotionally flooded, especially when confronted by a teacher, the child's thinking regresses to a form of irreversibility (Piaget, 1971a, 1971b). They do not think through the sequence of past actions and future consequences, but simply feel that they are in the spotlight and everyone is looking at them. As a result, they feel they must show their autonomy, no matter what. When flooded children are given commands, such as "Don't put your feet on the desk," what they often hear and remember is "feet on the desk." Unknowingly, the teacher may actually be suggesting that the child perform the very motor actions she does not want.

Words also trigger motor-meaning responses in children (Piaget, 1965). If a teacher is reading kindergartners a story that says, "The tiger growled and showed his ghastly teeth," a glance at the young audience will show most of the children "growling" and showing their teeth. Words suggest to young children a motor-meaning (Piaget, 1965) response that they impulsively seem unable to control. Therefore, telling a child a "don't" sentence that ends with an action word or motor meaning is likely to result in the child's performing the motor meaning of the last words. There are also some who believe that children under the age of seven cannot comprehend contractions such as "don't" (Bailey, 2000). Therefore, the goal is to tell the child what to do, not what *not* to do. In this way the teacher presents a real solution, telling the child what actions she wants and suggesting the motor meaning of the desired actions ("keep your feet on the floor").

The final difficulty with the "don't do so-and-so" approach is that if a child is motivated by the need for power, the child most likely will engage in a power struggle (Dreikurs, 1972). As a toddler, a child begins to test out his autonomy by attempting to get around limit setting by parents and other adults (Erikson, 1950). If this limit setting by adults is erratic and inconsistent, these children may come to the conclusion that "don't" really is a word that triggers a game of, "Let's see if the adult really means what she has said, or can I beat her and do as I wish?" The "don't" statement as a command on the TBC places the teacher's back against the wall, requiring an immediate confrontation or physical intervention with the child. This challenges the teacher's power, perhaps even forcing her to remove the child from the classroom. The goal in using and understanding the TBC is to grant the child maximum power to change his own behavior by beginning with a low-profile desist (Kounin, 1977) and then using a command; only when the teacher is unsuccessful in gaining compliance does she then gradually escalate the power until she gets results.

The Severity Clause and "Stop" Statements.   For every rule there is an exception. If the child is about to perform some action that is life threatening, is likely to produce injury, or will destroy expensive or irreplaceable property, the severity clause (Canter, 1976) applies. In such a case, the teacher states firmly or even shouts a "No, stop!" to attempt to get the child to immediately desist. The emergency requires an immediate motor action, and that is for the child to freeze or not move to touch the item he is approaching. If a teacher follows the rule above and regularly tells the child what to do, and not what *not* to do, an emergency "No, stop!" statement is more likely to be immediately obeyed. But if the child has an hourly diet of "don't do this, don't do that" and is told repeatedly, "No, don't do so-and-so" each day, he is desensitized to the prohibition contained in "No, stop!" statements and is less likely to immediately obey an emergency command. Save the "no" statements for when they are really needed.

Fighting Over Toys

Finally, the TBC can be used to guide the resolution between children who fight over toys and other possessions. Such fights are valuable teachable moments. Figure 3.2 shows panels of actions that normally take place as the teacher deals with such conflict.

Panels 1 and 2: We must have well-coordinated supervision to watch closely for such fights over toys. Tom wants Bill's toy and takes it.

Panels 3, 4, and 5: According to "Impulse Control as a Developmental Process" (see Figure 1.2), if Bill cannot use rational ability and language to retrieve his possession, he will respond with passivity, physical aggression, or verbal aggression. All of these flight-or-fight behaviors are developmentally nonproductive; the goal is to teach children to resolve conflict with language.

Panel 6: The teacher first must maintain her own emotional control, and STAR (smile, take a deep breath, and relax) permits her to do this. She also decides that Bill is the victim and the one with the immediate problem. The goal is to empower Bill by getting him to use language rather than passive or aggressive behaviors to resolve his problem. Out of a feeling of fairness, many teachers want to deal with or focus on Tom, the child who takes possessions from others. Tom needs to feel the power from his peers, not the grown-up teacher.

Panel 7: The teacher now is prepared to begin to use and move up the TBC, beginning with minimum power—looking—and then advancing to more controlling behaviors if Bill does not act. The looking involves closing space, with the teacher squared off and making unbroken eye contact with Bill, the victim. This is done at about three feet from Bill, or proxemics-near. If there is a danger of Tom or Bill running off and not wishing to deal with this situation, the teacher may hold Bill's left hand in her right, and Tom's right hand in her left. This physical closeness provides for the emotional closeness for real problem solving.

Panel 8: If Bill does speak up, we would skip to panel 13 and begin using the TBC's looking with Tom. If Bill still does not speak up, we move up the TBC to naming. The teacher verbally encodes or names Bill's feeling and/or the problem as she sees it. "You have lost your toy." If Bill is angry, this encoding may help Bill refocus on real problem solving and overcome his anger.

Panel 9: Again, without success with Bill, the teacher has had to move to questioning on the TBC: "What could you say to Tom?" The teacher's question is considered a verbal cue, encouraging Bill to think about what language response he could make. The teacher is granting him the autonomy and time to solve his own problem. With this questioning, the teacher does not necessarily want the child to respond to her, but rather she wants to produce a motor or verbal action in the child.

Panel 10: Without success, the teacher now becomes quite directive with Bill, giving a command ("Tell Tom . . ."), and providing the language model ("No, give it back"). This command is done with unbroken eye contact with Bill, by closing space and placing the teacher in proxemics-intimate, or face to face at six inches. In giving a command, the teacher has said Tom's name, gestured (pointing to the toy and then to Bill), and has told Bill what to do, not what not to do.

Panel 11: The teacher has now progressed across the TBC to acting, which requires some physical intervention. After all of the guidance and support

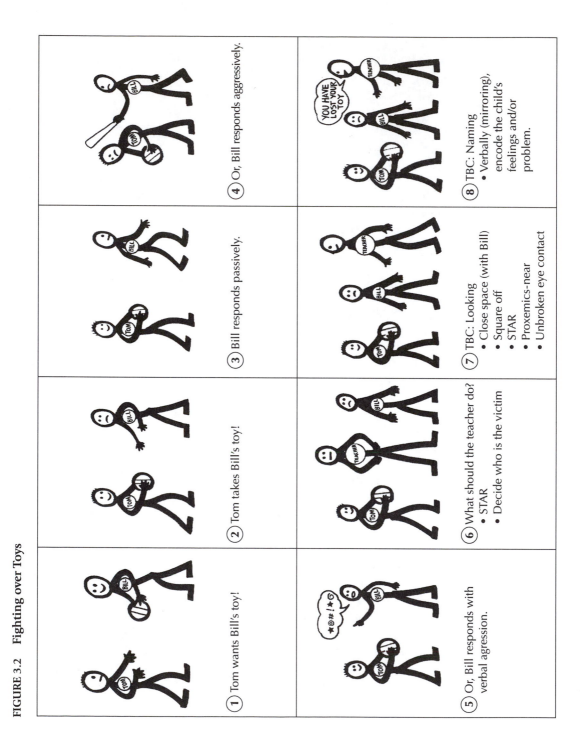

FIGURE 3.2 Fighting over Toys

1. Tom wants Bill's toy!

2. Tom takes Bill's toy!

3. Bill responds passively.

4. Or, Bill responds aggressively.

5. Or, Bill responds with verbal agression.

6. What should the teacher do?
   - STAR
   - Decide who is the victim

7. TBC: Looking
   - Close space (with Bill)
   - Square off
   - STAR
   - Proxemics-near
   - Unbroken eye contact

8. TBC: Naming
   - Verbally (mirroring), encode the child's feelings and/or problem.

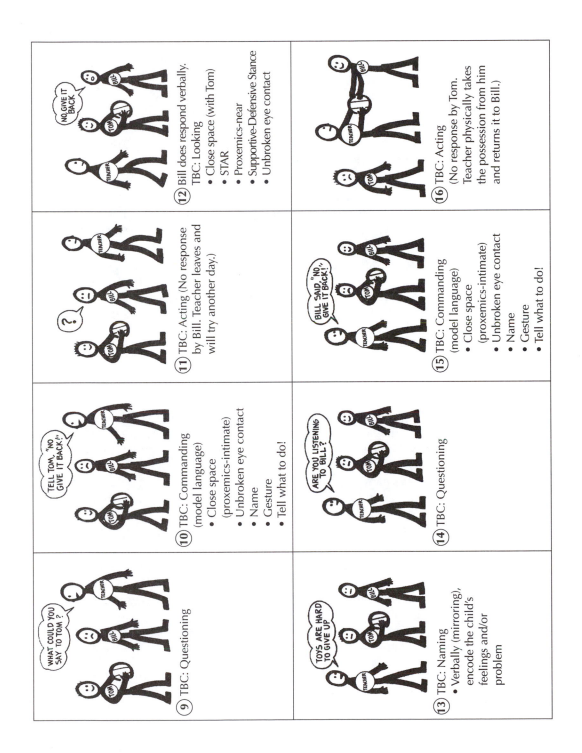

53

given to Bill, he still cannot use minimal language in this conflict situation. The teacher just departs, letting Tom keep the toy, and looks again for another time to facilitate Bill's assertiveness. Some passive children may have gained power by this nonresponse, possibly using water power by crying, having others rescue him by making others feel guilty through his sad appearance. Thus these passive-power children never need to grow, use assertive language, and become more socially competent. (Chapter 5 contains a host of intervention and facilitative techniques to use with Bill.)

This leaving action is unacceptable for some teachers, and they will say, "But Tom has learned that he can take things from others!" There will be many future teachable moments where Tom will clash with another peer. Also, other children are watching so they are also learning that the way to solve conflict is with language.

Panel 12:   If Bill does speak and use language—"No, give it back!"—then the focus changes from Bill to Tom. Tom needs to learn to listen and respond to his peers' communication. The teacher begins with looking, by closing space with Tom using proxemics-near. If she feels that Tom might be assaultive, she moves to a supportive-defensive stance. She makes unbroken eye contact with Tom, relaxes with STAR, and waits.

Panel 13 and 14:   If Tom does not return the toy, the teacher uses naming ("Toys are hard to give up"), and if need be, moves to questioning ("Are you listening to Bill?").

Panel 15:   Again, if Tom does not return the toy, the teacher uses a command, first repeating the language model ("Bill said, 'No, give it back.' ") and telling Tom directly, "Give the toy back." She accompanies this command with closing space—proxemics-intimate—with Tom, maintaining unbroken eye contact, stating his name, gesturing, and telling him what to do, not what *not* to do. She might repeat this command as a broken record three times, giving Tom some time to consider and act.

Panel 16:   After the broken record, the teacher acts by physically taking the toy from Tom and returning it to Bill. She must be careful because when she does this Tom might act out with kicking, biting, or grabbing. (Chapter Six describes how to deal with assaultive behavior.) She can also use the TBC to help Tom get started in some other activity. "Tom, you may be disappointed and angry that you must give back the toy (naming). What other things can you see to do in the room? (questioning). Tom, there are tricycles to ride, or you may sit and relax. Pick one and begin now (commanding)."

The confrontation between Jimmy and his teacher over the "paint sword" incident and conflict over possessions are examples of those myriad small desist requests—or teachable moments—that a classroom teacher faces daily in working with children. The incident is dealt with in a matter of minutes, and the teacher escalates up the TBC as she intervenes, modifying her approach as she receives—or fails to receive—certain responses. With some children, especially physically and verbally aggressive children, these teachable moments may arise five or six times in an hour and occur daily. The teacher may be required over many weeks and months to handle such incidents with one particular child. The many techniques found in the following chapters can be of great help.

Summary

When the difficult child is about to act out or to take some form of disruptive action, the questions are (1) what are the goals of the teacher when she intervenes, and (2) what actions should the teacher take? Using the construct developed in Chapter 1 (see Figure 1.1), the goal is to have students move to language and rational thinking (Social Self) to solve daily social conflict situations or use the productive language of play. The methods of intervention with such difficult children during these teachable moments include looking, naming, questioning, commanding, and acting (physical intervention) while granting the child the autonomy to reflect on his own behavior and make choices to change. Figure 3.4 shows this expanded continuum with a behavior under each larger category. (Note that acting with restraining and transporting an acting-out child will be covered in Chapter 4.)

FIGURE 3.3   Teacher Behavioral Continuum (TBC) (Expanded)

Looking	Naming	Questioning	Commanding	Acting

1. STAR
2. Proxemics
  · far
  · near
  · intimate
3. Stances
  (unbroken
  eye contact)
  · closing space
  · squaring off
  · supportive-
  defensive
	1. Active listening
	2. Door openers
	3. Acknowledg-
	  ments
		1. "Stop!"
		2. "What" questions
		3. Contracting
		  (How will you
		  change?)
		4. Relax chair
		  (if needed)
			1. Move to the
			  child, kneel
			  down to make
			  direct eye
			  contact
			2. State the child's
			  name
			3. Gesture
			4. Touch the child
			5. Verbally demand
			  that the child
			  stop
			6. Demand a
			  motor action
			  for positive
			  behavior by the
			  child (tell the
			  child what to
			  do, rather than
			  what not to do)
			7. Promise a
			  follow-through
			  consequence
				1. Restraining
				2. Transporting

REFERENCES

Alberti, R. E., & Emmons, M. L. (1975). *Stand up, speak out, talk back.* New York: Pocket Books.

Alberto, P. A., & Troutman, A. C. (1990). *Applied behavior analysis for teachers (3rd ed.).* New York: Merrill-Macmillan.

Bailey, B. (2000). *Conscious discipline: Seven basic skills for brain smart classroom management.* Oviedo, FL: Loving Guidance.

Bradshaw, J. (1990). *Homecoming: Reclaiming and championing your inner child.* New York: Bantam Books.

Canter, L. (1976). *Assertive discipline: A take-charge approach for today's educator.* Seal Beach, CA: Canter & Associates.

Canter, L., & Canter, M. (1992). *Assertive discipline: Positive behavior management for today's classroom.* Santa Monica, CA: Canter & Associates.

CPI-Crisis Intervention Institute (1987). *Nonviolent crisis intervention for the educator: Volume III, The assaultive student.* Brookfield, WI: National Crisis Prevention Institute.

DeVries, R., & Zan, B. (1994). *Moral classroom, moral children: Creating a constructivist atmosphere in early education.* New York: Teachers College Press.

Dreikurs, R. (1964). *Children: The challenge.* New York: Hawthorn/Dutton.

Dreikurs, R. (1968.) *Psychology in the classroom: A manual for teachers (2nd ed.).* New York: Harper & Row.

Dreikurs, R. (1972). *Discipline without tears: What to do with children who misbehave.* New York: Hawthorn Books.

Erikson, E. H. (1950). *Childhood and society.* New York: W. W. Norton.

Glasser, W. (1975). *Reality therapy: A new approach to psychiatry.* New York: Harper & Row.

Glasser, W. (1986). *Control theory in the classroom.* New York: Harper & Row.

Gordon, T. (1974) *T.E.T.: Teacher effectiveness training.* New York: David McKay.

Gordon, T. (1988). *Teaching children self-discipline: At home and at school.* New York: Times Books.

Jones, F. (1987). *Positive classroom discipline.* New York: McGraw-Hill.

Jones, F. (2001). *The tools for teaching.* Santa Cruz, CA: Fredric H. Jones and Associates.

Kounin, J. (1977). *Discipline and group management in classrooms* (rev. ed.). New York: Holt, Rinehart & Winston.

Piaget, J. (1965). *Moral judgement of the child.* Trans. M. Grabain. New York: Free Press.

Piaget, J. (1971a). *The construction of reality in the child.* New York: Ballantine Books.

Piaget, J. (1971b). *The language and thought of the child.* New York: World Publishing.

Wolfgang, C. H. (1996). *The three faces of discipline for the elementary school teacher: Empowering the teacher and students.* Boston: Allyn and Bacon.

Wolfgang, C. H. (2001). *Solving discipline and classroom management problems: Methods and models for today's teachers.* Boston: Allyn and Bacon.

Wolfgang, C. H., & Wolfgang, M. E. (1995). *The three faces of discipline for early childhood: Empowering teachers and students.* Boston: Allyn and Bacon.

SUGGESTED READINGS

Dreikurs, R., & Grey, L. (1968). *Logical consequences.* New York: Meredith Press.

Glasser, W. (1969). *Schools without failure.* New York: Harper & Row.

Glasser, W. (1978). *Glasser's approach to discipline.* Los Angeles: Educator Training Center.

Wolfgang, C. H. (1977). *Helping aggressive and passive preschoolers through play (5th ed.).* Columbus, OH: Charles E. Merrill.

Wolfgang, C. H., Mackender, B., & Wolfgang, M. E. (1981). *Growing and learning through play.* Poali, PA: Judy/Instructo.

Wolfgang, C. H., & Wolfgang M. E. (1992). *School for young children: Developmentally appropriate practices.* Boston: Allyn and Bacon.

CHAPTER 4

Dealing With the Acting-Out Child

Revengeful, assaultive, and acting-out children are simply reflexive beings; their negative behavior is automatically triggered by external stimuli or situations and by internal fears. To help such children requires strong controlling techniques, demanding that the teacher first set limits (as described with the use of the Teacher Behavioral Continuum in the preceding chapter) and then plan a systematic process to help them gain self-control and a reawakening sense of trust. To keep the child and others safe from the child's acting out and aggressive actions, the teacher may need to nonaggressively restrain the child.

There are generally four levels of crisis development leading to possible acting-out acts by the child:

Level 1: Potential Crisis

Level 2: Developing Crisis (a power struggle including ventilation and defiance)

Level 3: Acting-Out Behavior (assaultive/revengeful)

Level 4: Tension Reduction

These levels parallel the passive-aggressive construct explained in Figure 1.1. Consider how a teacher may respond to a student's aggression, again using Jimmy and the paint sword as an example:

Crisis Level 1: Potential Crisis

Jimmy stands before the paint easel. Using a large thick paintbrush, he dips the end into the paint pot. Soon the brush reappears, dripping with a large glob of paint. As a peer walks by, Jimmy turns and sticks out the brush as if it were a sword and attempts to "stab" his schoolmate. The peer screams and runs off, much to Jimmy's delight. A second child unknowingly wanders by, and Jimmy positions himself for a second attack.

The teacher STARs (smiles, takes a deep breath, and relaxes). She then moves to a supportive-defensive stance, having closed space standing at a proxemics-near position (three feet away). The teacher establishes unbroken eye contact.

TEACHER (*commanding*): "Jimmy, stop!" She points to Jimmy's brush and then to the paint pot and moves face to face with him. "Put the brush in the paint pot and go to the block room and find something to do there."

Jimmy stands, still holding the brush tightly with both hands, glares directly at the teacher, and then looks down at the floor.

TEACHER (*commanding*): "Jimmy, stop!" She places her hand gently on his shoulder. "Put the brush in the paint and go to the block room and find something to do there" (broken record).

Crisis Level 2: Developing Crisis

JIMMY: "You witch! You witch! Keep your hands off me! Keep your hands off me! No, let me go—don't touch me!"

The teacher lets 45 seconds pass. "Jimmy, stop! Put the brush in the paint pot! (broken record). If you cannot, then I will need to take the brush from you" (preparatory command—moves toward Jimmy).

Crisis Level 3: Acting-Out Behavior

Jimmy turns and, with both hands, including the one still holding the brush, forcefully pushes the teacher at waist level, making a large green streak of paint on her skirt and knocking her back three full steps; the teacher quickly catches her balance.

TEACHER (*commanding*): "Jimmy, stop. Put the brush in the paint and go to the block room" (broken record).

JIMMY: "No—let me go!"

Jimmy screams at full volume and again attempts to push the teacher with both hands; the teacher grasps both his arms at the wrist to prevent him. He drops the paintbrush and attempts to bite the teacher's right hand, which is holding his left wrist. To prevent this, the teacher pulls both of Jimmy's arms above his head and moves her hands away from his mouth. He now lashes out with his right leg in three quick kicking motions, one of which strikes the teacher squarely on the shin, causing her definite discomfort.

The teacher holds both of Jimmy's wrists in one of her hands. He kicks, missing contact with the teacher's shin. Seeing that a small side room is empty, she visually signals a coworker that she is departing and pulls Jimmy into the room and closes the door.

TEACHER (*naming*): "Jimmy, I am not going to hurt you, and I am not going to let you hurt me. You are safe—I will keep you safe, I will not hurt you!"

The teacher now releases Jimmy to see if he will quiet down; instead, he runs to the door to pull it open and run out. The teacher physically prevents this by holding the door. He kicks the door, to his discomfort, and runs his arm across the block shelf, knocking most of the blocks to the floor with a great crashing noise. He now moves to the window and violently strikes it with a fist; it cracks, but the windowpane stays intact. This action carries the real potential for Jimmy to injure himself, but before a second blow lands, the teacher again grasps his wrists and pulls and partially carries him to a chair, where she seats herself before an upright mirror. The teacher is now forced to use nonaggressive restraining techniques for Jimmy's own safety.

Seated *behind* the child, the teacher puts her arms around Jimmy, grasping his right wrist with her left hand and left wrist with her right hand and pulling him toward her in a way that causes the Jimmy's arms to cross over the front of his body (see Figure 4.1). The teacher moves her body sideways to the child on a 45-degree angle while seated on a small chair in front of an upright mirror. This places the child's back or hip on the teacher's right thigh, and she then pull his arms back toward her and lightly lifts up. While holding Jimmy in the basket-weave restraint (National Crisis Prevention Institute, 1968), the teacher parallels her physical action with accompanying verbal explanation and reassurance to Jimmy.

> **TEACHER** (*naming, now in a whisper*): "Jimmy, I am not going to hurt you, and I am not going to let you hurt me. You are safe—I will keep you safe. I will not hurt you! I am the teacher. I keep children safe; I will not hurt you! Jimmy, I am holding you with my hands to keep you safe. These hands will not hurt you. See . . . see . . . see in the mirror. You can see in the mirror that

FIGURE 4.1   Basket-Weave Restraint

I am not hurting you. You are safe. See my hands. They are holding you, but they are not hurting you." Jimmy attempts to struggle free, but the teacher holds him firmly in front of the mirror (Elkisch, 1957). "Look in the mirror. You can see in the mirror that I am not hurting you. You are safe. See my hands—they are holding you, but they are not hurting you. You need to be here on my lap until you can relax. I am holding you, but I am not hurting you!"

Jimmy attempts to bite the teacher again, but the teacher moves to prevent this; Jimmy screams a list of profanities at the teacher.

TEACHER (*naming, continuing to speak in a whisper*): "I am not going to let you hurt me, and I am not going to hurt you. Look in the mirror. You can see me, and you can see yourself. I am not hurting you. These are helping hands that do not hurt children! You are safe. I am going to keep you safe. I am the teacher. I am the boss, and I can keep children safe. I am going to keep you safe!" Jimmy now begins to cry and slowly stops struggling.

Crisis Level 4: Tension Reduction

TEACHER (*naming, points to Jimmy's image in the mirror*): "Jimmy, that is you, and I can see by your face that you are very angry. But look, here are my hands, and they are holding you to keep you safe. I will not hurt you—you are safe now." Jimmy's body goes limp in the teacher's lap. The teacher permits Jimmy to cuddle in her lap, and she reaches to the shelf to retrieve a children's book, which she reads to him in a soft, gentle voice (tension reduction).

This is one of the most demanding teacher-child interactions, one that involves a clear assault on the teacher and a danger to the child. When dealing with such a child, the teacher's heart is pounding and the adrenaline is pumping through her body, pushing her to a state of hyperalertness and creating a supportive-defensive stance for her own protection and, secondarily, for the child's safety. Out of her own understandable fright, she may emotionally flood, thus causing herself real difficulty in thinking correctly and acting constructively as these sudden incidents unfold.

Experts who have studied such acting-out actions by children recognize a general level-by-level progression in the child's behavior and actions. Teachers who understand these levels of crisis progression can better understand and be less frightened when these incidents occur. Previous thought rehearsal allows for constructive responses (see Figure 4.2).

Crisis Level 1: Potential Crisis

As a result of some source of frustration, the child appears as if he is a tightly wound spring ready to snap; emotional energy and tension are mounting. His hands may be clenched into a fist with white knuckles, and he may drop his eyes or glare intently, his gaze either focusing sharply on a peer or teacher or, instead, alternately focusing

FIGURE 4.2   **Levels of Crisis, Child Behavior, and Teacher Guidance**

Crisis Level	Student Behavior	Teacher's Goals and Techniques
1: Potential Crisis	As a result of some frustration, the child appears as if he is a tightly wound spring ready to snap. His hands may be clenched into a fist with white knuckles, and he may drop his eyes or glare intently, his gaze either focusing sharply on a peer or teacher or, instead, alternately focusing on his subject and then darting away. He may become physically restrictive, pulling inside of himself and turning away, or become active—pacing and exhibiting nervous tics. His actions clearly attract the attention of peers and observant adults. However, he is still rational.	The child, if caught quickly, is still rational enough to respond to teacher's language. Have the child ventilate through language (talk it out) or redirect the child to symbolic play (play it out). Redirect the child away from fluid materials and social interaction, giving him his personal space. If possible, make few or no demands. With the use of teacher's language, employ naming techniques. With symbolic play, channel the child's energy and aggression from the body to the toy, from the toy to play, and from play to work. Provide lap time if possible.
2: Developing Crisis	To maintain his power over a teacher or peer, the child now screams or shouts, using verbal aggression in the form of swearing or name calling, which appears to release or vent stored-up tension. This may quickly escalate to threats against peers and teachers and/or definite defiance of the teacher (regresses to the "doggie-horsy" brain).	The teacher positions herself in an alert supportive-defensive stance and permits the child's ventilation through verbal aggression. If the verbal aggression turns to defiance, the teacher moves to provide a command (assuring the student of potential consequences: "I will need to take the paint brushes away, and you will need to find another place to play.") and promises of safety. Give the child time and space to vent, and do not physically intervene if possible.
3: Acting-Out Behavior	The child now becomes totally revengeful and irrational, unable to control his own actions. He physically strikes out in a direct assault toward peer or teacher by choking, biting, or hitting/throwing (now in the reptilian brain).	In response to the assault, the teacher defends herself with restraining techniques (basket-weave restraint) and accompanies her physical actions with commanding and naming, sending two messages: an order to desist action in a way the teacher desires, and verbal reassurance through a promise of safety and nonaggression toward the child. Restrain the child in front of a mirror if possible.
4: Tension Reduction	After the violent action, the child is deflated and becomes passive with little energy (Inside Self). He has feelings of guilt and helplessness as to how others might respond to him. Intervene by mirroring both body referencing and motor imitations if the child retreats too deeply into passivity, such as sleep or physical self-abuse (moving back to the rational brain).	The teacher helps cognitively revisit the happenings for the child, first by having him talk about it using naming techniques and then, if unsuccessful, advancing to questioning.

on his subject and then darting away. He may become physically restrictive, pulling inside of himself and turning away or actively pacing and exhibiting nervous tics. His actions clearly attract the attention of peers and observant adults. Children will ask, "Why is Jimmy acting funny?" Adults, on the other hand, will say, "It looks like Jimmy is going to have one of his bad mornings." The child, if caught quickly, is still rational enough to respond to the teacher's use of language. The goal is to take this built-up internal energy and have the child ventilate it externally in representational form in two ways: through the use of language (talk it out) or through the use of symbolic play (play it out).

Talk It Out (Verbal)

If possible, the teacher brings into use the naming techniques learned in Chapter 3. "Jimmy, I can see that you are very unhappy this morning—tell me what is bothering you" (door opener). If the child does speak, the teacher uses acknowledgments and active listening and encourages the child to externalize or ventilate these strong, pent-up feelings through language and words. Some of these words may be aggressive and hostile. If this talking it out is effective and the child begins to reveal the root cause of his heightened emotional condition ("Andy won't let me play with him!"), the teacher might be able to help him resolve his problem or dilemma.

Reconsider the Jimmy example:

> **TEACHER** (*naming statements*): "Jimmy, paints can be scary, and sometimes hard to control. That is fun and exciting for you, but other children are frightened by the paintbrush."
>
> **JIMMY:** "I don't like him!" Jimmy is referring to Walter, who just passed by and was the target of Jimmy's latest attempt to stab with the paintbrush.
>
> **TEACHER:** "You're angry with Walter?" (active listening)
>
> **JIMMY:** "He is mean!"
>
> **TEACHER:** "Walter has been mean to you?"
>
> **JIMMY:** "Yes, I am his best friend, and he let Robert sit next to him at snack!"
>
> **TEACHER:** "You're angry because you were not able to sit by your friend." (active listening)
>
> **JIMMY:** "Yes, could I sit by Walter?"

The teacher's efforts to determine the cause of Jimmy's sword play have exposed a deeper problem that Jimmy is facing, and she can begin dealing with it from a new perspective: problem solving.

> **TEACHER** (*defining the problem*): "Ah, you have a problem, and that problem is, how can you get to sit next to Walter at lunch? Let's think together of ways that you might solve this problem. What are your ideas?" (generating possible solutions)
>
> **JIMMY:** "I could get to the table first."
>
> **TEACHER:** "That may work, but let's think of a lot of other ways, too."

JIMMY: "I could ask Walter to sit by me. But Robert always gets there first. I could sit at the little table [which has only two seats] and ask Walter to sit with me. But Robert would come and push me out of my seat. I could push him back or tell the teacher on him!"

TEACHER: "Robert wants to eat with Walter, too." (active listening)

JIMMY: "Yes, could he eat at the little table? We could have three chairs and be best friends."

TEACHER: "Which one of your ideas is best?" (evaluating the solutions)

JIMMY: "Having three chairs."

TEACHER: "Is that what you will do at lunchtime today?" (deciding which solution is best)

JIMMY: "Yes."

The next day, the teacher watches as Jimmy adds a third chair to the table and invites both Walter and Robert to eat with him (implementing the solution). After lunch the teacher talks to Jimmy.

TEACHER: "Was your solution to your problem a good one?" (evaluating the solution)

JIMMY: "Yes, it was *great*, and I figured it out all by myself!"

With quick and early intervention, the teacher has headed off an aggressive situation with this child by having him talk it out through language, with the teacher using naming techniques.

Play It Out (Motoric to Symbolic)

If the root of the child's stress is beyond the immediate and manageable confines of the classroom setting, such as having been paddled by daddy at breakfast that morning, the teacher would not be able to turn to problem solving but would instead continue with active listening or move to the second method of ventilation through symbolic play.

With the use of play materials, the teacher may redirect and encourage the child to vent motorically (bodily) stored-up energies, which later will lead to symbolic play. This follows a line of development from the body to the toy, from the toy to play, and from play to work (Freud, 1968).

Body to Toy. The child who is actively pacing is directed to a free space where others will not interfere with his actions. "Jimmy, I see this morning that you are going around and around. Here, use this toy car (wheeled toy),* and make it go

---

*The size of the wheeled toy will depend on the amount of space available to be sectioned off as a private space for the child. Very large wooden trucks and cars (six to eight inches or bigger) might be effective in a large-muscle room or playground but generally not in a well-balanced indoor space. A very small wheeled toy could be confined to a very narrow space such as a table top or large cafeteria tray with raised edges, which helps establish control of error (see Chapter 6, Degrees of Freedom and Control of Error, for definition).

around and around." The teacher barriers or sections off this zone, possibly with movable partitions or chairs, to give Jimmy private space and encourage him to externalize his pent-up energies into "car pushing"—from the body to the toy (Freud, 1968). This car pushing initially will be aggressive, with the car smashing into things. The barrier of private space has clearly defined a zone where the aggression is acceptable. Also, a child in Crisis Level 1 becomes overly sensitive when others—peers or teacher—move into or invade space around him within a zone of three to six feet. The teacher prevents classmates from going into this space because the flooded child will feel threatened by their approach and may assault the unsuspecting peer. This aggressive car play is exactly what is wanted because it gives a motoric outlet (Body Self) to Jimmy's emotional energy (Inside Self), and the child might play aggressively with the car (Outside Self) for minutes, hours, or even days. The teacher continues looking and maintains modality prompting with the child, indicating nonverbally to him that she approves of this aggressive play. If the child takes his aggressive car play outside of the defined area established by the teacher, she redirects him back to the defined space. If he again fails to stay within this space, the teacher is now required to stay in the space with him. The child may *not* use the toy, such as the car, to take aggressive actions against others but must play in the make-believe miniature world of toys (micro-symbolic play).

Biting, Spitting, Hitting, and Kicking.   The teacher attempts to move the child who is a biter from biting to playing with a miniature lion puppet, alligator puppet, or tiger that has an open mouth and teeth (see Figure 4.3). She encourages him to play motorically, performing the act of biting within the miniature world of toys (micro), but not with peers (see Figure 4.4): "People are not for biting, but make-believe biting with the lion is okay."

Spitting is aggression or assault with the mouth, so the same aggressive mouth-and-teeth animals and channeling would be used with the biting child. Fluid materials often frighten the spitter, so fluids with fewer degrees of freedom, such as clay and modeling dough, are more effective with him. Teacher structuring into more open fluids (to be described in Chapter 6) may also be appropriate.

For the child who hits and kicks, energy may be channeled into the motoric action of carpentry construction play, such as pounding a nail into an old log or sawing discarded wood pieces, or more controlled fluid construction (pounding clay or modeling dough).

Indeed, the goal is to actually encourage the child to bite, hit, and be outwardly aggressive—but to channel that energy and action through a socially acceptable outlet as motoric play and to confine it to the miniature world (micro) and in a clearly defined and sectioned-off space where this aggressive play may occur. Thus, the aggression is channeled and, again, aggression is energy misdirected.

Applying the Teacher Behavioral Continuum (TBC)

Toy to Play.   The teacher closely watches Jimmy's aggression or similar actions by other children who are biting and hitting. She uses micro toys (such as the wheeled toy,

FIGURE 4.3   Body to the Toy (Lion): Channeling Aggression

the alligator or tiger puppet, and the modeling clay) and then begins using the TBC to channel the aggressive toy action (Outside Self) into real symbolic play (Social Self).

Looking.   By looking approvingly, the teacher signals that the child is encouraged to play aggressively with the toys and materials, but within the established space. She may accompany the child's strong emotional ventilation by using naming statements.

FIGURE 4.4   Channeling Aggression

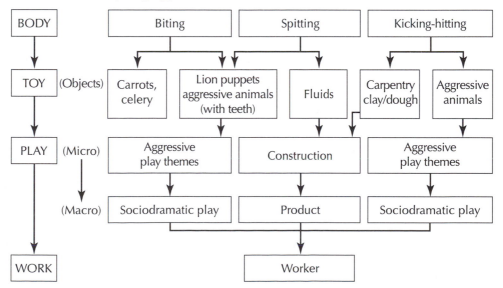

Naming.   "Jimmy, I see that your car [alligator puppet, tiger, modeling dough, or hammering] is very angry and it crashes [bites, is squashed, hits] into everything." This verbal encoding of the child's nonverbal actions applies emotional words to the child's actions with toys and materials, and the teacher may repetitively mirror the child's motor actions and ventilation (Peller, 1956; Axline, 1971) with naming for minutes, days, or weeks. She judges the amount of energy expended, and when she feels that enough energies have been ventilated or expelled, she moves to a more intrusive intervention, using questions and attempting to have the child move to play.

Questioning.   "Jimmy, I see you going around and around. Where is the road for your car? (The teacher pushes unit blocks toward the child.) Where is a garage for your car? Where is the gas station for your car to get gas?" The questions attempt to have the child mentally reflect on more positive play and dramatic themes as he plays with the vehicle.

For the alligator puppet or aggressive animal play, the teacher may ask, "Could your alligator [or toy tiger] keep the people safe and be a mommy or daddy to the other toys?" For the pounding of carpentry or using fluids such as clay, the question might be, "Could you make something with your hammer and nails [clay, etc.]?" When the child responds by stopping the aggressive use of the toys and materials and appears interested, the teacher may give him some wait time to see if he can produce symbolic play on his own; if it becomes apparent that he cannot play but is interested in the suggestion, the teacher moves to commanding.

Commanding.   "Jimmy, pick up the blocks and move them to create a road for your car! Use these small blocks to make a gas station. Make a story happen with your toys!" (For the carpentry, she could direct, "Make an airplane," or for clay, "Make an egg for a bird's nest" or similar object.) If there still is a lack of direction and initiative but an apparent interest, the teacher now moves to acting.

Acting.   By acting, the teacher actually takes the toys and models the play activity for the child. "Jimmy, watch what I am doing. I am putting these long blocks in line to create a road, and we can run the car down the road like this [teacher demonstrates]. Now, we will use these little blocks to make a house for the car to live in—a garage for the car." The teacher physically handles and moves the objects, performing the play that she is verbally describing.

The teacher now begins to retreat down the power levels of the TBC.

> TEACHER (*commanding*): "Jimmy, you play what I played. What else can you do with the toys? (questioning) Oh, I see, you are pretending to fill the car with gas" (naming). Finally, with the child engaged in successful play, the teacher retreats to looking as she modality prompts her approval of the child's play actions.

Play to Work.   If the child's actions do explode, for example, in an attempt to bite someone, the teacher may physically inhibit him and point out to him the realities of this situation: "I cannot let you hurt others, and I will not let others hurt you."

The teacher may then channel the aggressive actions of the child into a socially acceptable outlet. Normally, this is from body-aggressive actions to a toy or object (Freud, 1968). In working with the child who attempts to bite another, after she states, "I cannot let you bite others, and I won't let others bite you, " she can add, "Here, you may use the lion [or alligator] puppet to pretend to bite these toy people." The teacher then gives the child a puppet with a large, fierce mouth and encourages him to demonstrate his aggression on the microcosm of small toys (see Figure 4.5). With the micro toys, the child first pursues aggressive themes, and when using the fluid materials the child pounds and uses them aggressively. Finally the child moves to symbolic play and making a product, which leads to becoming a cooperative worker with others.

The mastery of aggression is a developmental line from the body to the toy, from the toy (object) to play (symbolic fantasy play or construction as in making products), which moves from microcosmic play (play with little toy figures) to macrocosmic play in the form of sociodramatic play with peers. Finally, from the mastery of aggression through play (sociodramatic play) with peers, the child can become a cooperative socialized child whom we may call a worker (Freud, 1968). The child as a cooperative worker can inhibit his childish desires to destroy and gain immediate gratification of his own needs and delay his self-centeredness for the good of the social task that the group is attempting to accomplish. Thus, through play, the child gains direct improvement in his ability to master the larger life space full of others.

Lap Time

There are certain times during Potential Crisis in which the teacher may offer her lap to the child for purposes of cuddling. Jimmy has awakened at 6:00 A.M.; confusion reigns in the home of his large family. He fought with his sister in the car on the way to school this morning and has been spanked by his mother. He enters the school or center "wired," definitely within the realm of Potential Crisis. The teacher says, "Jimmy, I can see by your face this morning that you could use some lap time. Come sit here on my lap and let me read you your favorite book." Lap time or cuddling permits the child to positively regress into himself (Inside Self) and relax, thus getting out of a tense, hyperalert, defensive frame of mind (Body Self). However, many children cannot be touched while in Potential Crisis and will assault the teacher if she approaches and invades his private space. With such children, the teacher should extend open arms to the child and have him come to her to be cuddled; if instead she goes to the child, he may see it as a potentially hostile or aggressive approach and react negatively.

Further guidelines while the child is partially flooded and in the Potential Crisis stage include (1) redirecting the child away from highly fluid materials, such as sand—especially in large sandboxes—water play, and painting (Chapter 5 includes techniques for introducing these more expressive fluids to the difficult children) and (2) preventing or limiting social interaction with others, giving the child his private space. Symbolic play channels the child's energy and aggression from the body to the toy, from the toy to play, and from play to work, and cuddling the child if he will accept it helps get him relaxed.

If the teacher is unsuccessful in resolving the problem in Potential Crisis because she caught it too late or the intensity of the child's emotional flooding was excessive, most likely the child will regress to a more severe Crisis Level 2: Developing Crisis, with its two substages of ventilation and defiance.

Crisis Level 2: Developing Crisis

To maintain his power over a teacher or peer through a sense of fear, the child enters Developing Crisis. He uses ventilation, or verbal aggression, in the form of screaming or shouting, swearing, name-calling, and similar verbal outbursts. This verbal aggression, no matter how it frightens classmates and the teacher, is a good release. When a child ventilates in this manner, the teacher should *do nothing*. She does not challenge the child as he screams, shouts, and swears because, after many minutes of doing so, the child will no longer have energy left for a physical assault. So the longer the child ventilates by being verbally aggressive, the better because he simply is wearing himself out and dispersing his stored up tension. The teacher should not be frightened by the verbal aggression, but she should be cautious. This verbal aggression may quickly escalate into threats to peers and the teacher and/or definite defiance toward the teacher.

> JIMMY (*screaming*): "You witch! You witch! Keep your witch hands off me! Keep your witch hands off me! No, let me go—don't touch me!" (ventilation)
>
> JIMMY (*screaming*): "No, my brush! I am going to kill you!" (defiance)

In this Developing Crisis situation, the child is not rational and has regressed to the "doggie-horsy" brain, ventilating by shouting, much like snapping and snarling. While in this state of extreme agitation, the child will have much difficulty in hearing the teacher's words but will visually assess her nonverbal actions for any hint of action toward him, which he will interpret as hostile and aggressive. Once the defiance and threats are heard, the teacher should signal to a fellow adult or send another child to get another adult—in short, get help. This second adult is helpful both in restraining the child and as a later witness to any actions that may occur in the event of any administrative evaluation. Also, the teacher should take actions to remove onlookers by either having the other children moved to another room, sectioning the area off from the view of other children, or, if possible, moving the child to another room. Witnessing an outburst by the revengeful, flooded child can be very frightening for classmates, and witnessing the teacher's restraining actions on the assaulting child can appear to young children as if she is hurting this child.

When the Developing Crisis event does occur, there are two ways of responding: with commands and with a supportive-defensive stance. Commands and a supportive-defensive stance should be used with flooded, revengeful children who may pose a danger to themselves or others or to objects. Commands are made up of two parts: a verbal command and a follow-up preparatory command given as a choice, if the child does not desist. One more important verbal statement should be said repetitively as a broken record: a promise of safety.

> **TEACHER** (*naming—promise of safety*): "Jimmy, I am not going to hurt you, and I am not going to let you hurt me. You are safe—I will keep you safe. I will not hurt you, and I will not let others hurt you. I want to help you be safe!"

The nonverbal actions that are a part of the command and supportive-defensive stance differ dramatically, but the manner in which commands are delivered should have certain common characteristics. While issuing a command, the teacher should use a well-modulated voice (controlled tone, volume, and cadence)—neither too fast nor slow, neither too loud nor soft (National Crisis Prevention Institute, 1968); in the most normal voice possible, the teacher tells the child the motor actions or behaviors that she wants performed. Remember, she does not tell the child what *not* to do.

> **TEACHER** (*commanding*): "Jimmy, stop!" The teacher points to Jimmy. "Put the brush in the paint pot." She moves face to face (proxemics-near, eye contact). "Go to the puzzles, and select one—or go to the beanbag chair and relax with a book."

Giving the child a choice between two actions is an attempt to still grant the child some autonomy, and the teacher will be less likely to get a refusal.

The parallel nonverbal behavior, or stance, of the teacher to accompany the command is to gesture with the hands and fingers, move squarely in front of the child and make fixed eye contact, and touch the child. When accompanying the verbal assertive command, these actions are most confrontational. By these actions, the teacher challenges the child's power directly. Commands, with the accompanying stance, may be used effectively with a child who is motivated by attention getting and power seeking and who may be having an uncontrollable moment. However, this approach will be disastrous with the revengeful child who is flooded and has taken this general position toward his world. Do not use a command with a flooded, revengeful child at Developing Crisis because the challenge will set him off, and he will assault the teacher, especially if she violates his personal space.

The teacher technique to be used with children at this level of crisis is the supportive stance. The nonverbal behavior used in the supportive-defensive stance includes the following:

1. Standing still and not getting closer than three feet from the child. There is no touching the child, for this would be considered an invasion of his private space, or bubble. All people have a circle of space around them, a hypothetical bubble, and they feel unsafe if others close into this space. When others do close into this space, it is typically for purposes of expressing affection (cuddling) or for purposes of aggression. The hyperalert Developing Crisis child

will clearly interpret closing space as an aggressive act, which will arouse his aggressive instincts. This is why even with a child in Potential Crisis, the teacher signals the child to come to her to cuddle rather than approach the child to cuddle.

2. Turning the body at an angle, with the preferred foot pointed toward the child and the other foot at a 45-degree angle. The teacher should not put herself squarely in front of the child. This angled stance toward the flooded child is interpreted as nonhostile, while squaring off is a face-to-face position for confrontation and fighting. The foot pointed toward the child may be raised to deflect or block the kicking action of a child's foot. The other, angled foot can be used for temporary balance; a stance with parallel feet leaves the teacher flat-footed and prone to being knocked off balance by any minor assault.

3. Establishing eye contact, which should not be fixed or glaring.

4. Placing the teacher's hands so that the child may see them and so that the hands are ready to block an assault (but without gesturing or making any threatening moves with the hands, such as pointing). If assault appears imminent, the teacher should hold both hands open, one at stomach level and the other in front of her chin, with the palms up. The teacher also should not put her hands on her hips, clench her fist, or point.

While employing the supportive-defensive stance, the teacher states a supportive verbal command and repeats it two or three times, attempting to have the child hear it. If she does not get a change in the child's behavior, she clearly states a preparatory directive statement for possible consequences, followed by a promise of safety.

> **TEACHER:** "Jimmy, lower your voice, put the brush in the paint pot, and go to the block room." (Commanding—the teacher is also in a supportive-defensive stance.) "Lower your voice, put the brush in the paint pot, and go to the block room. (broken record) If you do not, I will ask you to put the brush in the paint pot, and go to the puzzles and select one—or go to the beanbag chair and relax with a book. Jimmy, I am not going to hurt you, and I am not going to let you hurt me. You are safe—I will keep you safe. I will not hurt you, and I will not let others hurt you. I want to help you be safe!"

The standoff between the flooded Developing Crisis child and the teacher's supportive demand and stance should not be rushed. The goal is to prevent an assault by the child. The teacher may permit many minutes to go by in hopes that the child will desist, back down, and comply. If he does not and instead regresses further, the next action is likely to be physical flooding and an assault or acting-out behavior.

Crisis Level 3: Acting-Out Behavior

The child now becomes totally revengeful and irrational and cannot control his own actions (has regressed to the reptilian brain). He physically strikes out in a direct assault against a peer or teacher by choking, biting, kicking, grabbing, or hitting/throwing.

In response to the assault, the teacher should defend herself with the restraining techniques described below (using the help of a second adult if one is nearby). The teacher should accompany her physical actions with a command, sending two messages: a directive for the child to calm himself and a promise of safety and nonaggression toward the child. The teacher should perform the restraint in front of a mirror if possible.

Basket-Weave Restraint

If the child is small enough and the teacher has the advantage of strength over him, she may choose to use the basket-weave restraint. This is the preferred restraining technique because the teacher may use a mirror from a seated restraining position. This physical restraint is accomplished by the teacher's getting behind the assaulting child and putting her arms around him, grasping his right wrist with her left hand and his left wrist with her right hand, and pulling toward her in a way that causes the child's arms to cross over the front of his body (see Figure 4.1). As she stands, the teacher moves her body sideways to the child, her feet at a 45-degree angle. This places the child's back on her right hip. She then pulls his arms back toward her and lifts up. This causes the child's heels to come slightly off the floor, forcing him to stand on his tiptoes with his weight supported by her thigh. The teacher also may hold or restrain the child in a seated position. The teacher should use the minimal amount of force needed so that no injury is done to the child. The basket-weave restraining hold is the preferred hold with very young children because of the reduced likelihood of injuring them.

The teacher must accompany physical restraining with naming ("You are very angry"), a command, and a promise of safety ("I am not going to hurt you").

> **TEACHER:** "Jimmy, I want you to stop hitting and relax. (commanding) When you do so, I will let you go! (preparatory command) You are safe. I am not going to hurt you, and I will not let you hurt me!" (promise of safety)

The entire verbal sequence is repeated over and over—like a broken record.

Some early childhood teachers state that when they are hit, kicked, or bitten by a child, they hit, kick, and bite back, so that the child "knows how it feels." **A teacher should not *ever*, under any circumstances, hit, kick, or bite a child in response to the child's actions.** This could rightly be defined as child abuse, and the teacher could properly be charged under the law. When a young child is flooded and carries out an assault, he is no longer rational and capable of stopping himself; returning his aggression does not teach him how it feels but simply confirms his unreasonable concern that the teacher is a person to fear. By using nonviolent restraining techniques, parallel supportive commands, and promises of safety, the teacher does *not* return the child's aggression. In this way, the teacher gradually gains the child's trust. During each of these crisis levels—and especially during the assault action—the child is terribly frightened. He actually scares himself when he is out of control.

The teacher must be careful not to overuse restraining and transporting techniques that require the physical holding of the child. These are high-risk actions when done incorrectly and can bring injury to the child or even to the teacher. Restraining is used only when the child's acting-out behavior is endangering himself or others, or the potential exists for the destruction of expensive property. Transporting is used after the child has calmed down as a result of being restrained but may act out again, and/or the child is located in such a space that if he does act out there is potential of injury, such as during a field trip in a location where the child might run into a busy street.

If the child becomes passive or introverted after an assault, retreats to a protective corner or space out of the way of the classroom activities, and now presents no danger to himself or others, the teacher should simply leave him alone and consider him to have moved to Crisis Level 4: Tension Reduction.

Crisis Level 4: Tension Reduction

After acting out, the child is deflated and becomes withdrawn, with little energy. He has feelings of guilt and feels helpless as to how others may respond to him. Some children retreat so far back into passivity (Inside Self) that they fall asleep or begin self-abusive activities, such as pulling out their hair, biting themselves, or some similar act of physical abuse on themselves. If the child retreats too deeply into passivity or begins physically self-abusive activities, the teacher will intervene with mirroring both body referencing and motor imitations. (See Chapter 5 for details on mirroring.)

At the Tension Reduction stage, the child is now rational, and the teacher can try to help him cognitively recall what has happened, for he may not actually remember what started the flooding incident or what occurred once it began. This involves use of the TBC techniques.

> Jimmy slouches down into the chair, drops his eyes, pouts for a period of four to six minutes, and then begins to sit up in the chair and watch the other children.
>
> The teacher makes eye contact and seats herself knee to knee to the child (proxemics-near).
>
> TEACHER (*naming*): "Jimmy, you had a very scary morning. I need to talk to you about the painting. What did you do?" (questioning)
>
> JIMMY: "I don't know." (Or the child might say, "I painted people!")
>
> TEACHER (*commanding*): "Well, I saw what you did, and you were using the paintbrush to paint Mark. What is the rule about how paints are to be used?"
>
> JIMMY (*eyes drop*): "A-a-h, keep the paint—ah—paper."

TEACHER (*commanding*): "Yes, when paints are used, our rule is to keep the paint on the paper. Also the rule is that hitting and biting are not allowed, and when someone is angry they need to use words to tell the other person. When you got angry and started hitting and biting, I needed to hold you tightly to keep you safe. I did not hurt you, and I didn't let anyone hurt you. I kept us both safe. These are helping hands, not hurting hands, and these hands keep children safe." The teacher restates the rule so it is very clear. "Now you and I must work this out. We must have an agreement." (contracting)

The teacher moves to Jimmy, takes him gently by the hands, and makes eye contact. "What will you do to change? When you use the paints again, how will you use them?" (questioning)

JIMMY: "Keep the paint on the paper."

TEACHER (*questioning*): "Yes. Do we have an agreement on this? Can I depend on you to remember the rule?"

JIMMY: "Yes." Jimmy looks up and makes eye contact with the teacher.

TEACHER (*questioning*): "What will you do when someone makes you angry?"

JIMMY: "Words."

TEACHER (*contracting*): "Good, we now have an agreement. If you agree, I want to shake hands to show a special agreement between us." The teacher holds out her hand to Jimmy and smiles warmly. Jimmy returns the teacher's smile and shakes her hand.

TEACHER (*commanding*): "If you can now remember the painting rules, you may paint. But if you forget the painting rules, your behavior will say that you do not know how to use paints and you will not be able to use them. Now, you can come back to work and play with us, when you feel that you are ready."

Jimmy hops up, takes off the paint smock, hangs it on the appropriate hook, moves over to the puzzle shelf, and selects a puzzle.

It is recommended that during Tension Reduction, the child and teacher be eye to eye in a very close, intimate space. This can be done by seating the child on an adult chair, with the teacher sitting on a small child-size chair, or by placing the child on a counter top with the teacher standing, thus bringing them eye to eye.

During Tension Reduction it is important that the child be able to cognitively state—or for the teacher to describe—the events that occurred in a way that imparts no guilt. The relationship between the teacher and child needs to reach a new emotional state free of hostility. Both the child and the teacher need this reunion.

The teacher should not force a verbal apology from the child. The verbal statement may be something the teacher may want, but if it is forced the child will begin to have feelings of guilt. If the Tension Reduction goes well, the child will have feelings of remorse and may wish to apologize, but he may express it in nonverbal form. There is a feeling of warmth, and the child physically leans into the teacher for a small cuddle, or the child meets the teacher's eyes, saying nothing but smiling affectionately. These signs are better than a forced apology. If a teacher was actually physically hurt, she must also learn during the interaction to express nonverbal forgiveness through cuddling and smiling, but she must also do it in the form of verbal expression as a statement of a promise of safety.

Classmates As Onlookers to an Assault

It has been suggested that steps should be taken to remove onlookers by either having the other children move to another room, sectioning an area off from the view of other children, or, if possible, moving the acting-out child to another room. Witnessing the revengeful, flooded child is very frightening for classmates, and seeing restraining actions on the assaulting child may appear to young children as if the acting-out child is being hurt.

It is important for the teacher to deal with the classmates who were onlookers to an assault by the acting-out child. Witnessing such aggression can cause an individual child or an entire group of children to move to Potential Crisis, in which they become highly anxious with accompanying behavior that might escalate through these crisis levels. The teacher may deal with this by doing the ventilating techniques previously suggested in working with Potential Crisis children. The teacher should now view the entire class, after these acting-out incidents, as being in Potential Crisis; she should encourage the other children to play it out or talk it out. The play-it-out technique (motoric ventilation) involves having each child take the inner tension and disperse it from the body to play, while enabling children to talk it out (verbal ventilation) involves holding one or more class problem solving meetings, using the naming techniques.

Motoric Ventilation

When dealing with many children who are experiencing fears and inner tension, the teacher should stop any close, socially demanding indoor play and instead (if practical) take the entire class outside. This gives children plenty of space to be motorically active, with much running. It would be advisable *not* to take children to activities that immobilize their bodies or demand close cooperation, such as at the snack table, nor should they be encouraged to lie on their cots or mats soon after viewing a frightening action. If a teacher takes the flooded children into these activities without permitting an opportunity for ventilation, she will find large numbers of these young children unmanageable.

The running off of tension will work with most children, but the outdoor supervision will require extra vigilance because of a dramatic increase of fantasy role play related to aggressive roles. Play with such characters as Ninja Turtles and Batman will be seen. These roles are acceptable outlets for the children in a large outdoor space, but there must be close supervision by the teacher to make sure that the pretend aggression does not take over the children and that they do not begin to kick and strike one another. Just as the teacher is required to use the TBC to facilitate the play of an individual child progressing along the construct of body to toy, toy to play, and play to work, she may need to channel this outdoor play for many children from negative, aggressive theme play to more positive, constructive role play.

Although this intervention may be needed, the teacher does want to permit as much harmless aggression as possible because it provides good ventilation. She should intervene only with those children who overstep and cannot control the aggressive play to the point where they actually do become aggressive. She can also expect to witness much silliness and nervous, giddy laughter among the children, as they appear to run wild on the playground.

Verbal Ventilation

The entire class is seated in a circle on child-size chairs. The assaulting child is included in the meeting, and should preferably be seated in the lap of a teacher's aid or assistant teacher. Just as the questioning techniques were used in Tension Reduction to enable the teacher to establish an emotional equilibrium with the acting-out child, they are needed to reestablish equilibrium with the child's classmates. They have seen or heard the frightening event and have identified themselves as a part of the action. Through verbal ventilating in a class meeting, the teacher attempts to reach the point where she and the children have gotten rid of any feelings of hostility. If she does not do this, the other children—out of their fear of the acting-out child—will begin to make him the outside aggressor (Isaacs, 1972) by refusing to play with him, shunning him, or even acting aggressively toward him.

Here's how a class meeting might unfold. Notice that the teacher begins with naming or active listening with its accompanying techniques, and then moves to questioning.

> **TEACHER:** "I would like to talk about some scary and frightening things that happened this morning." (door opener)

No one speaks for a few minutes, but then a discussion begins.

> **HARRIET:** "Jimmy was mean!"
>
> **PAUL:** "He hits people."
>
> **TEACHER:** "Jimmy was very angry. And when he gets angry, he hits." (active listening)
>
> **DIANA:** "I don't like him, he is mean!"
>
> **TEACHER:** "When people hit, it is hard to like them."
>
> **JOHN:** "You hurt Jimmy's arm."
>
> **TEACHER:** "When I held Jimmy, you thought I was hurting him." (active listening)
>
> **PAUL:** "You didn't hit Jimmy."
>
> **TEACHER:** "What else did you see and feel?" (door opener)
>
> **NANCY:** "I saw Jimmy hit you and bite your arm. He cried and screamed naughty words."

This verbal ventilation may continue for five to ten minutes, with the teacher maintaining naming techniques. Now the teacher moves to questioning and does not hesitate to deal with the realities of the situation and explain misinformation.

TEACHER: "What happened first . . . Harriet?"

HARRIET: "Jimmy was splashing people with paint. He wasn't using the rules for painting."

TEACHER: "What happened next?"

JOHN: "You told Jimmy to stop painting, and he pushed you and got paint all over your dress."

TEACHER: "What happened next?"

DIANA: "Jimmy screamed and hit, and you took him into the block room. And there was a big crash."

TEACHER: "What happened next?"

PAUL: "You hurt Jimmy's arm."

TEACHER (*commanding*): "No, because Jimmy got so mad that he could hurt me, others, or himself, I needed to hold him tightly to keep him safe. I am the teacher and boss but I do not hurt children. I am a friend, but when children get very angry I need to hold them tight to keep them safe." The teacher gives a reality explanation and a promise of safety.

PAUL: "You hurt Jimmy's arm."

TEACHER (*commanding*): "No, Paul, I was holding his arm and hands tightly so that his hands would not hurt me. I did not hurt Jimmy. I was keeping him safe. Come up here, Paul." Paul stands before the teacher. "Let me show you how safely I was holding Jimmy." The teacher now demonstrates the basket-weave restraint on Paul and two other children. He giggles as if it is a game, and now a number of other children want a chance. The teacher demonstrates the basket-weave restraint on all children who have requested it—including Jimmy, who has left the assistant teacher's lap.

TEACHER: "When friends get very angry, they sometimes try to hurt other people. I am the boss, and I keep people safe. And no matter how mean people are, I will not hit them, I will not hurt them, I will not kick them, and I will not bite them. I am the teacher and I hold children to keep them safe." The teacher gives another reality explanation and promise of safety. "Now we need to make some promises. We need to have an agreement. What should we do when others make us angry?"

Nearly the entire class, in unison: "Use words."

TEACHER: "Yes, when others make us angry, the rule is that we do not hit, but we tell that person with words, and we can come to the teacher to get help. Hitting, biting, kicking, and spitting are against the rules. Also, how can we help Jimmy when he gets mad?"

DIANA: "We can share with him."

JOHN: "We can let him play with us."

TEACHER: "We now all have an agreement. We are going to use words when we are angry, and we are going to invite Jimmy to be our friend and play with us." (contracting)

This example, of course, is designed to model teacher techniques and is certainly somewhat artificial. This ventilation process and the confronting and contracting might take many minutes, or even many meetings, and it may need to occur throughout the year if aggression is high in the classroom. But the techniques to be used and the general attitude and processes to be employed, should develop in a direction much as the one demonstrated in this example.

This class meeting serves a number of purposes. First, it ventilates any pent-up anxiety and feelings that any child might have after witnessing aggression. Second, it helps both Jimmy and his classmates to reduce tension, potentially preventing him from becoming the object of their aggression. Third, it helps children understand that if they, too, should become angry (and they will), the teacher will not take aggressive action against them but instead will help. Fourth, it dispels any misinformation and misperceptions the children might have ("You were hurting Jimmy's arm").

Summary

At times teachers are faced with a child who is so flooded that he acts out in a manner that endangers others and himself. Teachers are required to understand the levels of crisis through which the child will move and first make attempts to get the child to ventilate his inner tension through language or play that will move from the body to the toy, from the toy to play, and then through play to become a cooperative worker. Teachers also will be required to mediate for classmates who have witnessed acting-out behavior through classroom meetings.

REFERENCES

Axline, V. M. (1971). *Play therapy* (6th ed.). New York: Ballantine Books.

Elkisch, P. (1957). Psychological significance of mirror. *Journal of American Psychoanalytical Association, 5,* 235–244.

Freud, A. (1968). *Normality and pathology in childhood: Assessments of development.* New York: International Universities Press.

Isaacs, S. (1972). *Social development in young children.* New York: Schocken Books.

National Crisis Prevention Institute (1968). *Nonviolent crisis intervention for the educator: Volume III, the assaultive student.* Brookfield, WI: National Crisis Prevention Institute.

Peller, L. E. (1956). Libidinal phases, ego development and play. In *Psychoanalytic Study of the Child, 9* (pp. 65–92). New York: International Universities Press.

SUGGESTED READINGS

McMurrain, T. (1975). *Intervention in human crisis.* Atlanta: Humanics Press.

Wolfgang, C. H. (1977). *Helping aggressive and passive preschoolers through play.* Columbus, OH: Charles E. Merrill Publishing.

Wolfgang, C. H., & Wolfgang, M. E. (1992). *School for young children: Developmentally appropriate practices.* Boston: Allyn and Bacon.

5 Teaching Positive Social Behaviors Through Play

The knowledge and constructs developed in the first four chapters can now be used to create a guidance or teaching program for passive and aggressive preschoolers. To review, here are the relevant constructs:

- the concept of Inside Self (passivity), Body Self (physical aggression), Outside Self (verbal aggression), and Social Self (ability to play)
- the social stages (unoccupied, solitary, onlooker, parallel, associative, and cooperative)
- the definition of play (sensorimotor, symbolic, and construction)
- play materials (micro and macro symbolic toys, fluid construction, and structured construction)
- the Teacher Behavioral Continuum (TBC) in limit setting and interaction with the child (looking, naming, questioning, commanding, and acting)

Creating a guidance or teaching program for passive and aggressive preschoolers can be done generally in three ways or some combination of the three:

1. *One-to-One Facilitation:* Passive and aggressive children can be pulled out from their normal classroom activities for a prescribed series of facilitation procedures carried out by a skilled teacher. This would depend on the classroom having a second or third teacher, assistant teacher, or aid, but it may be justified because the aggressive child is so destructive to the classroom that the teacher is spending nearly all of her time focusing on the difficult child, or the passive child may be so introverted that the short in-class facilitation produces little to no result. This one-to-one facilitation may take place while other students are on the playground, leaving the classroom free, or the teacher may use the floor of a small office or storeroom as a facilitation play space containing micro symbolic toys (small people, toy furniture, animal figures, and so on), fluid materials (paints, clay, and paper and crayons) and structured construction materials (Legos and puzzles), along with a freestanding movable mirror.

2. *Group Facilitation:* The teacher can, during normal classroom activities, bring together a small group (four to six children) of well-functioning and playing

children with the targeted passive or aggressive child as a group member and use the peers as good models for demonstrating the activities that the teacher is initiating. This permits the teacher to continually supervise all children and remain in the classroom.

3. *Teachable Moments Facilitation:* Once the teacher becomes skilled in facilitation techniques, she can target the difficult child for short periods of time during the normal school day and then move on to other children that are actively playing. These short teachable moments, involving only one or two minutes of facilitation, will accumulate and over time will begin to help the difficult child progress through the facilitation steps, thus helping the child to become more productive socially. There also will be well-functioning children who for short periods of time show characteristics of aggression or passivity; this same method may be used with them as a part of the normal routine of the day.

Finally, the skilled teacher may wish to use each of the three methods, that is, taking the difficult child out of the classroom for a one-to-one facilitation, working with him in a group, and then finding short periods of time to work with him during the normal classroom play period.

Facilitation

The theoretical foundation of the facilitation techniques that follow is built on the premise that there is a universal "railroad track" of development that all children must follow in the first three years of life as they gain the ability to become cooperative, socially skilled individuals (Mahler, 1970; Mahler, Pine, & Bergman, 1975). Passive and aggressive children have been unable to progress developmentally down this track and are stalled or frozen in their development, performing ritualized response behaviors to their classroom world—a life-stance position (Harris, 1969)— of passive or aggressive behavior. The aggressive and passive children might be three, four, five, or six years old, but they may act as if they are ages one or two.

The steps and techniques that follow are drawn from the interaction between the child and caregiving adult (usually the mother) during the early stages of development through which most children normally progress (Mahler, 1970; Mahler et al., 1975) and gain social skills. In a very broad sense, the techniques attempt to "remother" the child, helping to create the security and behavior that will jump-start the child's development.

The plan of action, or directional road map, for helping passive and aggressive young children generally progresses through the following steps to help the child establish the following:

Step 1: Bonding (basic body trust)
Step 2: Causal action toward others
Step 3: Causal action toward objects

Step 4: Causal action and the expression of ideas and feelings through symbolic play

Step 5: Causal action with coplayers

Caution: Some physical aggression by children has a medical basis, and their doctors might put them on medication to help control their behavior. While such medication may aid in setting a climate for controlling the child's behavior, it is suggested that, if the child does not receive the following facilitation (or similar social facilitation), the behavior will return once the medication is removed. Such children need to learn and be taught developmentally appropriate social skills. It is also suggested that, as teachers intervene with these children in cooperation with the parent and doctor, medication may be gradually withdrawn.

As discussed in Chapter 1, it is strongly recommended that children with difficult behaviors first receive a full medical examination. Hyperactivity, aggressiveness, and self-abuse may be symptoms of a treatable medical condition. Once all possible medical causes have been eliminated, it is recommended that children receive a full examination from a developmental clinic. Teachers should maintain communication with these professionals, and parents should be fully informed.

Step 1: Bonding (Basic Body Trust)

It is from birth to age eight months that the newborn child gains a basic sense of trust or mistrust (Erikson, 1950) about his world and himself. Through caring, parents bathe the child in sensory experiences related to modalities of touch (caressing), hearing (singing and play-speaking), seeing (peek-a-boo games), smell (a pleasing perfume or food smells), and taste (through feeding). All of these modalities result in close physical bonding and attachment. Because senses are the channels to experiencing the real world, these same sense modalities can be punished as a result of negative sensory experiences, developing a sense of mistrust. The child whose hands are smacked when he touches items that are forbidden by the caregiver* will come to mistrust his world. The act of touching and being touched emotionally floods or panics the child, and he withdraws from physical cuddling or the touching of sensory materials such as finger paints and clay.

A child who is screamed at incessantly by adults may panic when hearing various sounds and will cup his ears with his hands to shut out the sounds of the world, or he may need to fill his world with sound and cannot stand quiet (as with the child who continues to make odd noises at rest time). A child with a punished vision

---

*Caution: These limited examples describe parental activities, but there could be many reasons outside the control of the parent for the same punished modality. For example, a two-year-old child at a restaurant accidentally pulls a coffee pot off a counter and burns himself, causing second- and third-degree burns; as a three- and four-year-old, he demonstrates much fear in finger painting or water play. The accident happened beyond the control of the parents, and they are not the cause of this behavior.

FIGURE 5.1   Normative Developmental and Facilitation Stages

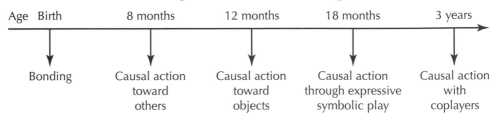

Age	Birth	8 months	12 months	18 months	3 years
	Bonding	Causal action toward others	Causal action toward objects	Causal action through expressive symbolic play	Causal action with coplayers

modality may not be able to meet adults or peers eye to eye, possibly the result of having been confronted by adults and told, "Look me in the face," but then slapped with a warning of, "Don't you look at me that way, young man!"

Some of these punished sense modalities and the aggressive and passive behaviors may not be the result or the fault of the early caring adults (early mothering), but might be the result of the child's genetic makeup (born with some abnormality), neonatal experience (seen in "crack" babies or other chemical insults or imbalances during pregnancy), or birth process. One aggressive child was born with the placenta (birth cord) around his neck; another sustained head bruising and possibly a lack of oxygen in the first few minutes of life. This oxygen deprivation may have caused some early brain damage. Both of these children were difficult infants and showed much aggressive and violent behavior as three-, four-, and five-year-olds.

In contrast, most children have a strong modality or cluster of modalities that can be used to give them comfort and reassurance (Winnicott, 1971). Some children can relax at nap time by having their back rubbed, others are comforted by being talked to softly or listening to soft music, and others want to be held firmly and cuddled. If the teacher carefully watches the interaction between the child and the primary caregiver, especially as the child is learning to first adapt to the new and strange classroom, she will see the child's mother prompting the child's best modality (looking, speaking [sound], or touching) to give the child comfort. The teacher may now prompt the child in a similar manner. In contrast, if the child cannot relate physically, and his new teacher pushes herself on him in an attempt to comfort him—especially approaching the child in his weak or punished modality—the child will flood, panicking at the physical intrusion or advance.

In the bonding (or rebonding) step, we ask, "Can the child meet us eye to eye and communicate verbally or nonverbally?" "Can the very difficult child physically cuddle with the teacher?" "Does this child socially/emotionally attach and interact confidently with the teacher and peers?" For the misbehaving aggressive or passive child, the answer is clearly no.

For most normally developing children, this bonding is well established during the first year of life. When a newborn baby is hungry, cold, and in a general state of displeasure, a caring adult (usually a parent) appears visually before the child to feed, diaper, cuddle, and emotionally comfort him. These pleasurable or comforting feelings enable the young infant to become attached and bonded to the adult, and especially to the adult face (Mahler, 1970; Mahler et al., 1975). The typical social-emotional interaction between the infant and primary caregiver is eye-to-eye facial play that can be seen in games of peek-a-boo, "this little piggy went to market," blowing "raspberries" on the child's tummy, and a host of similarly joyful facial play, all of it involving eye contact between the child and the significant caregiver. The misbehaving child is not bonded, and therefore the teacher's first step is to establish eye contact with the child and establish a bonding relationship between the teacher and child.

The passive child is withdrawn into his Inside Self (see Chapter 1) and appears to be cut off from his sensor modality, appearing expressionless and glassy-eyed and retreating into his own internal world. This passive child is literally pulled around by his parents or his peers from place to place and appears to be adrift in the sea of activity around him—he does not seem to see or participate. The passive child does not seem to have needs or to express his needs and take action to have them fulfilled. He appears helpless and cannot be the cause in his world. When cuddled by an adult, he does not reject the advances as an aggressive child might, but he does not cuddle back. When a child has a "poor attention span," it means that the child perceptually has retreated into the Inside Self and appears to be unaware of the outside, social world. Mirroring activities attempt to reach the child in his internal world and draw him out.

For the aggressive child, who lives most of the time in the Body Self (see Chapter 1), perceptions and senses are turned outward. The aggressive child is aware, but this awareness is at the hyperalert level. The aggressive child is overwhelmed by sensory input—visual stimuli, sound, and touch. Characteristic of many aggressive preschoolers is their inability to cuddle and accept physical affection or touch. When an adult touches some of these aggressive children, it is as if her touch is burning them—they may have a punished tactile sense. Other "punished" modalities may be shown, such as vision, when the child refuses to make eye contact.

Establishing Eye Contact (Visual)

The procedure for establishing eye contact with a target child is to bring the child before a large, upright, freestanding or wall-mounted mirror. The child should stand between the teacher's legs or should sit on her lap to cuddle (if the child *will* cuddle; if not, the following techniques will teach the child to cuddle). The teacher and the child both face the mirror. The child's back is to the teacher, who is looking over the child's shoulder, able to see him face to face. The mirror might be positioned approximately two to three feet away from the child; the teacher then gradually moves herself and the child closer and closer to the mirror, thus narrowing the child's personal space. The teacher now uses a token reinforcer (such as a Post-it note or any other item that sticks to the mirror's surface) paired with a primary reinforcer or reward (something edible). In using a note as a token, the teacher starts with bright, dramatic colors, such as hot pinks, and progresses to lighter, less dramatic colors, ending up with white or tans (fading of intensity). The note can be stuck anywhere on the mirror, as the teacher attempts to get the child to take the note and give it to her in exchange for a reward (possibly a raisin or piece of oatmeal cookie).* It is, of course, important that the reward be a positive reinforcer for the child, and it may take some experimentation to find one that will work. The reward also must be something that is easily handled, takes only seconds to consume, and will not satiate or quickly fill the child up. The process of taking and giving to the teacher requires the child to visually stand in front of the teacher and sets up a give-and-take sequence.

The teacher then turns the process into a game; she is animated and dramatic, as if this is the greatest game ever invented. The note is placed by the teacher on the mirror and the child physically retrieves it, gives it to the teacher, and then receives the reward. Thus, the teacher develops a mirroring game. The teacher may even initiate a game of hide-and-seek by sticking some notes behind the mirror, enabling the child to find them easily. The interval of rewarding is at first one to one: Each time the child retrieves a note and gives it to the teacher, a reward is given. After establishing this behavior four to six times, the teacher begins thinning the primary reinforcer by giving the reward only after two and then three retrievals. The task has taught the child to look out and visually find and locate an object (much like the mother's peek-a-boo play with an infant—lost and found). The use of the note is only one way that this mirror game can be accomplished, and the teacher should use her creativity in devising a host of similar playful activities. The central goal is to begin to have the child visually attend to the teacher and to overcome the punished sense of vision.

Group Facilitation

The mirror play can also be done in a group facilitation process in the classroom. The teacher simply takes a rectangular or half-round table and places it against the wall on one side. Then an upright, freestanding mirror is laid sideways at the back of the table and against the wall for support. Now if four to six children take chairs before the table, with the target child in the middle and standing between the legs of the teacher, the teacher can see the entire group in the mirror and the same mirror game can be done as explained above, but this time in a group with the well-functioning children providing models.

Child Body Referencing

Next the game is replayed with the teacher placing the note on the child's body, first on his extremities and then gradually moving toward his face. The child is encouraged to locate the token by looking in the mirror at his own body. For example, it may be placed in the following sequence:

On his foot (shoe)
On his knee

---

*I have generally rejected the behavioral techniques in early chapters, but the alert reader will see that I am now using behavioral techniques. These techniques are being used *only* to desensitize the modalities; Freudians or some developmentalists may be happier (and this is an attempt at humor) in wishing to view these techniques as recapitulating the early oral needs.

On the back of his hand

On his elbow

On his shoulder

On his chest

On the top of his head

On his forehead

On his cheek

On his chin

On his nose

It is important that each time the child pulls the note from his body part (or the teacher's body part, as suggested in the next procedure), the teacher labels the body part for the child. "Oh, Larry, you found it, it's on your nose" (the TBC naming function). Many difficult children have a limited or absent true concept of self, and this verbal encoding or labeling of their body is a beginning step in helping them gain an understanding of themselves. Also, the child is learning body parts that will be words and labels to be used in later steps in the facilitation process, when he learns the aspects of causality. This task has taught the child to visually scan and locate an object related to his own body through the mirror.

Teacher Body Referencing

The game is now played for the third time with the teacher sticking the note on her own body. She begins with body parts that are in front of the child (feet, hands, and knees—remember that the child is either in her lap or standing between her legs) and then gradually moves to parts of her body behind the child that he can see only by looking at the mirror. Finally, she places the note on her face. Places to stick the note on the teacher's body might progress as follows:

On her shoe

On her knee

On the back of her hand

On her forearm

On her elbow

On her shoulder

On the top of her head

On her forehead

On her cheek

On her chin

On her nose

This mirroring game may need to be played with the child—especially the passive child—for many weeks. Again, as this game is carried out, the teacher begins withdrawing any reward. The teacher should also withdraw the use of the note by gradually cutting the paper into smaller and smaller pieces and moving from bright colors, such as hot pink, to lighter and lighter colors, finally ending with white or light tan. The target behavior in Bonding is to use many days or weeks of facilitation, through the use of facial play with the mirror, to get the child finally comfortable with looking at the teacher's face and making eye contact. In this way, the teacher may attain one of the first steps toward having the child bond with her.

Touching and Cuddling

Most well-functioning young children can cuddle and give and accept platonic physical affection from significant adults in their lives, but most likely the physically aggressive child will become tense and rigid, physically rejecting affection. It is as if his tactile body trust is missing, and he acts as if physical touch is punishing or hurting him. Later, after the teacher has intervened with this child, he will appear as if he is "sticky," needing to constantly be on the teacher's lap and to constantly be physically comforted. In essence, after facilitation, it will appear as if the child is making up for lap time he may have missed during earlier stages.

For the passive child, cuddling with the teacher generally can be described as holding a rag doll. When we hug or cuddle with another person, we usually feel that person affectionately cuddling back, but the passive child typically does not give back. He responds as if he were a rag doll or wet noodle. It is as if the child is not even connected to his own body. It is through cuddling and a host of other interactions with the child's primary caregiver (mother/father) that the child attaches or bonds with the first significant adults in his life. These bonded, intimate relationships with meaningful adults in the child's life are basic to his development, but the passive or aggressive child has not bonded or has bonded poorly. The teacher's goal in the Bonding process is to intervene through modalities to build on nonverbal communication with the difficult child and then take actions to desensitize those punished modalities, permitting the child to fully experience his world in a relaxed, trusting manner.

The Facilitation Criteria Checklist (see Figure 5.2) shows the possible steps in a shaping process in which the teacher uses primary reinforcers and, through associative learning, pairs the primary reinforcer with the social reinforcers of being read to, being touched and cuddled, and hearing the teacher's words and phrases. Through the pairing of primary and secondary reinforcers, the child is learning to be comfortable, or is bonding, with the teacher and learning to cuddle and be touched. This is only one example demonstrating how to desensitize the touching or tactile modality. In similar manner, any other modalities that the child appears to be incapable of or uncomfortable in using freely or in a trusting way can also be reinforced (see Figure 5.3 for suggested sensory reinforcers) in the same manner.

FIGURE 5.2   Facilitation Criteria Checklist

Child's Name _____

Teacher's Name _____

School _____

Dates (write date)

1st week _____   5th week _____

2nd week _____   6th week _____

3rd week _____   7th week _____

4th week _____   8th week _____

At the end of each week of facilitation, rate the child on the following variables:

Behavior criteria	Yes	No	Sometimes
Step 1: Bonding			
1. Looks, finds, gives token from mirror	____	____	____
2. Looks, finds, gives token from child's body	____	____	____
3. Looks, finds, gives token from teacher's body	____	____	____
4. Looks at teacher's face when spoken to	____	____	____
Step 2: Causal Action Toward Others			
5. Permits teacher to be seated nearby (within three feet)	____	____	____
6. Permits teacher to be seated side by side	____	____	____
7. Permits teacher to place her hand on back	____	____	____
8. Permits teacher to place her arm around child	____	____	____
9. Will sit in teacher's lap	____	____	____
10. Feels relaxed when seated in teacher's lap (cuddles)	____	____	____
11. Touches most body parts (self) upon command to do so	____	____	____
12. Touches most body parts (teacher) upon command to do so and knows:	____	____	____
shoes (feet)	____	____	____
knees	____	____	____
backs of hands	____	____	____
arms	____	____	____
elbows	____	____	____
shoulders	____	____	____
top of head	____	____	____
forehead	____	____	____
cheeks	____	____	____
chin	____	____	____
nose	____	____	____
13. Can imitate teacher's body actions (open/close mouth, blink eyes, etc.)	____	____	____
14. Can imitate hand actions to "Thumbkin"	____	____	____
15. Can say and imitate hand actions to "Thumbkin"	____	____	____

(continued)

FIGURE 5.2   Facilitation Criteria Checklist (*continued*)

Behavior Criteria (continued)	Yes	No	Sometimes
16. Says name of body part to which teacher points:			
shoes (feet)	_____	_____	_____
knees	_____	_____	_____
backs of hands	_____	_____	_____
arms	_____	_____	_____
elbows	_____	_____	_____
shoulders	_____	_____	_____
top of head	_____	_____	_____
forehead	_____	_____	_____
cheeks	_____	_____	_____
chin	_____	_____	_____
nose	_____	_____	_____
Step 3: Causal Action Toward Objects			
17. Can place hands on back of teacher's hands while teacher paints	_____	_____	_____
18. Smears with object (stick) in finger paints	_____	_____	_____
19. Smears with one finger of each hand	_____	_____	_____
20. Smears with full hands	_____	_____	_____
21. Can smear over surface area larger than 1 by 2 feet with control	_____	_____	_____
22. Paints a symbol	_____	_____	_____
23. Is comfortable (not overly sensitive) to:			
classroom sounds (auditory)	_____	_____	_____
smells (olfactory)	_____	_____	_____
sight (vision)	_____	_____	_____
touch (tactile)	_____	_____	_____
Step 4: Symbolic Play (Micro)			
24. Does dramatic (fantasy) play with:			
miniature life (micro toys)	_____	_____	_____
gestures, sounds, or verbalization	_____	_____	_____
a theme (nonaggressive)	_____	_____	_____
Step 5: Becoming a Coplayer			
25. Functions:			
onlooker	_____	_____	_____
parallel	_____	_____	_____
associative	_____	_____	_____
cooperative	_____	_____	_____
26. Sociodramatic play:			
imitates a role	_____	_____	_____
makes believe with objects	_____	_____	_____
makes believe with actions/situations	_____	_____	_____
persists in play (10 mins.)	_____	_____	_____
interacts with others	_____	_____	_____
has verbal exchanges	_____	_____	_____

Helping a Child Learn to Cuddle.   The teacher must use her own personality, warmth, affection, and sense of caring to gradually make advances toward the physically rejecting child's ability to accept the teacher's cuddling. Here is an example of one teacher's progress.

1. While being read to, Tracy permits the teacher to be seated on the floor three feet from him for a period of three minutes. (The child is eating his favorite snack—primary reinforcer.)*
2. While being read to, Tracy permits the teacher to be seated on the floor three feet from him for a period of five minutes.
3. While being read to, Tracy permits the teacher to be seated on the floor six inches from him for a period of five minutes.
4. While being read to, Tracy permits the teacher to be seated on the floor and touching shoulder to shoulder for a period of three minutes.
5. While being read to, Tracy permits the teacher to be seated on the floor and touching shoulder to shoulder for a period of five minutes.
6. While being read to, Tracy permits the teacher to be seated on the floor with the teacher's arm across his back in a cuddling position for a period of three minutes.
7. While being read to, Tracy permits the teacher to be seated on the floor with the teacher's arm across his back in a cuddling position for a period of five minutes.
8. While being read to, Tracy permits the teacher to be seated on the floor with the teacher's arm across his back in a cuddling position and Tracy seated on the teacher's lap for a period of three minutes.
9. While being read to, Tracy permits the teacher to be seated on the floor with the teacher's arm across his back in a cuddling position and Tracy seated on the teacher's lap for a period of five minutes.

The preceding description is given as a model of how the teacher may plan elements of the facilitation strategy. Figure 5.3 provides other suggestions of desensitizing other modalities.

Step 2: Causal Action on Others

The difficult child—passive or aggressive—ritualistically acts the way he does as a defensive stand toward a world that scares him. The passive child has regressed to the Inside Self and the aggressive child to the Body Self (see Chapter 1). When objects

---

*The judgment as to whether to give a primary reinforcer will depend on the teacher's analysis of the responsiveness and effectiveness of the procedures, but the teacher will quickly initiate a goal of thinning and withdrawing reinforcers. The teacher may choose to use a different primary reinforcer.

FIGURE 5.3   Suggested Methods for Desensitizing Modalities

The teacher may need to do desensitizing activities with a difficult child who may have a punished modality. This is a list of items that have been successfully used in the desensitizing process by other teachers.

Steps	Modalities				
	Sight *(visual)*	*Touch* *(tactile)*	*Hearing* *(auditory)*	*Smell* *(olfactory)*	*Taste* *(gustatory)*

Step 1: Bonding	flashlight
	 mirror
	 pinwheel
	 colored lights
	 bubbles
	 reflector
	 strobe lights
	 Christmas tree
	   ornaments
	 wrapping paper
	 rubber worms
		balloons
		 wind fan
		 electric fans
		 air from hair
		   dryers (on
		   low setting)
		 body lotion
		 electric
		   massager
		 body powder
		 feather duster
		 water
		 sand
		 burlap
		 Silly Putty
			mother's voice
			   on audio
			   tape
			 party blowers
			 push toys
			 whistles
			 bells
			 wind chimes
			 tambourines
			 harmonica
			 car keys
			 kazoo
			 bike horn
				garlic clove
				 vinegar
				 coffee
				 perfume
				 cinnamon
				 suntan lotion
				 oregano
				 after-shave
				   lotion
				 flowers
				 vanilla extract
					fruit juice
					 flavored gelatin
					 raisins
					 cereal
					 honey
					 pickle relish
					 peanut butter
					 toothpaste
					 lemon juice
					 bacon bits
					 apple butter

and people make any demands on these children, the children are not confident and do not know how to "be the cause" or make the world meet their needs. Therefore, they have a behavioral vacuum (Alberto & Troutman, 1990). The life stance position of the passive child is one of helplessness and a feeling of unworthiness, while the motivation of the aggressive child is revenge—"the world has hurt me, and it is a frightening place; I will fight back and hurt others before they hurt me." In Bonding, the teacher began to establish the difficult child's trust at a very basic body level by having the child attach to her and by desensitizing modalities that may have been punished. With minimal trust beginning to be established, the teacher may now begin techniques found under Step 2 by beginning to teach the child to initiate and take action—to be the cause of actions that will occur and affect himself and others.

The teacher continues with the mirroring activity as described in Step 1, with the child in her lap or standing between her knees while both are in front of an upright mirror. There are three new goals in Step 2: (1) to have the child gain an awareness of self through motor action and labeling of his body parts; (2) to have the child learn to imitate the teacher's actions; and (3) to teach the child to initiate actions for the teacher to follow, thus having the child become the cause of an action. (Normally, older infants ages eight to twelve months are learning these goals of self-awareness and causality.)

During the notes game in Step 1, the teacher verbally encoded by labeling the child's body parts as well as her own. She now asks the child to show her the teacher's foot (knee, arm, elbow, shoulder, and so on) by having him touch that part. If the child fails to respond, the teacher needs to use either a primary reinforcer or a token that the child can turn in for a reward. Alternatively, she may need to back up and return to the procedures described in Step 1. The teacher needs to use her judgment and the learning procedure until the child can effectively show through touching that he knows all the parts of the teacher's body mentioned in Step 1. The teacher does a similar process with the child's body as a reference, having him touch his own body parts.

The mirror activity also is used to teach the child to imitate. In all of the imitative games that follow, certain actions will occur.

- First, the teacher provides the lead or model for the child as to how to perform the imitation, using the teacher's body. The teacher performs imitative activities (open/close the mouth, open/close the eyes, shake the head to the right, shake the head to the left, touch the top of the head, open and close the hands, and a host of any other imitative body actions). The child is then taught to imitate these simple actions. Again, reinforcers, such as edible rewards, may be used to get the child to perform this behavior.
- Second, the child performs the behavior (open/close his mouth, etc.) while the teacher imitates the child's actions—at a very basic level, he is nonverbally being the cause through imitation of the teacher.
- Third, the child learns to imitate by model using traditional hand games often used in early childhood classrooms. "Ten Little Indians" or "Thumbkin" are examples (see Figure 5.4). Again, the child is further developing the skill of learning to be the cause with these games, which requires language output accomplished by motor actions.
- Fourth, the child now plays imitative games to get the teacher to follow or imitate him. With the attainment of this skill, the teacher has made quite a large advance in teaching and establishing a sense of causality for the child.

What is important in the mirroring and imitative activities is to have the passive and aggressive child initiate the game, or be the cause, while the teacher follows. It is important that these games are a fun and joyful activity, and the hope is that the child gets caught up in the fun of the activity, as most well-functioning children would. What might appear to be a nonsense game is in fact an initiating activity for the child, allowing him to be the cause with language and, symbolically, with his hands (for example, pretending to wear grandma's glasses).

Being the Cause Through Language

The teacher may now return to the body-labeling mirroring game by asking the child to choose one of the teacher's body parts while she says its name. This simple activity requires the child to initiate the action motorically—the first rudimentary acts of

FIGURE 5.4   Imitative Body-Hand Games

Little Boy
Here's a little boy
(child makes a fist with thumb extended)
That's going to bed.
(covers fist with his other hand)
Down on the pillow
He lays his head.

He wraps the covers
*(second hand closes around first, letting thumb
    be exposed)*
Around him tight.
And that's the way
He sleeps all night.

Grandma's Glasses
Here are grandma's glasses.
(child uses fingers to make glasses over eyes)
Here is grandma's hat.
(two index fingers make pointed hat)
Here's the way she folds her hands
(fold hands and lays them in lap)
And lays them in her lap.

Grandpa's Glasses
Grandpa lost his glasses.
(fingers make glasses over eyes)
Before he went to bed.
Guess where grandma found them?
Right on top of grandpa's head!
(move glasses on top of head)

Mr. Bullfrog
Mr. Bullfrog sat on a big old rock.
(child makes a fist with thumb up)
Along came a little boy
(other hand walks)
Mr. Bullfrog KERPLOP!
(both hands slap knees)

Touch and Clap 1-2-3
Hands on your hips, hands on your knees.
Now put them behind you if you please!
Then on your shoulders, then on your nose.
Touch your eyes, then touch your toes.
Hold your hands high up in the air.
Then down at your side, now touch your hair.
Hold your hands high up as before.
Now let's clap, 1-2-3.

Thumbkin
(child holds both hands behind back)
Where is Thumbkin? Where is Thumbkin?
Here I am, here I am.
*(brings out one hand showing thumb; brings
    out the other)*
How are you today, sir?
(wiggles one thumb)
Very well, I thank you.
(wiggles other thumb)
Run away. Run away.
*(puts one hand behind his back, puts the other
    hand behind his back)*
Where is Pointer? Where is Pointer?
*(brings out hands with raised index finger,
    one at a time)*
Here I am, here I am.
How are you today, sir? Very well, I thank you.
(wiggles one index finger, then the other)
Run away. Run away.
*(puts one hand behind his back, then the other;
    repeat as follows for three remaining fingers)*
Where is Tall Man? Where is Tall Man?
Here I am, here I am.
How are you today, sir? Very well, I thank you.
Run away. Run away.
Where is Ring Man? Where is Ring Man?
Here I am, here I am.
How are you today, sir? Very well, I thank you.
Run away. Run away.
Where is Pinkie? Where is Pinkie?
Here I am, here I am.
How are you today, sir? Very well, I thank you.
Run away. Run away.
Where is the family? Where is the family?
(child brings out hands with all fingers extended)
Here we are, here we are.
How are you today, sirs? Very well, we thank you.
(wiggles all fingers on one hand, then the other)
Run away. Run away.

Pig
I had a little pig
(child makes a fist with thumb up)
And I fed it in a trough
(makes a cup with other hand)
He got so big and fat,
(makes circle of arms)

FIGURE 5.4   Imitative Body-Hand Games (*continued*)

That his tail popped off!
(clap both hands and knees)
So, I got me a hammer
(one hand is hammer)
And I got me a nail
(hammer on thumb of other hand)
And I made the pig
(continue to hammer)
A wooden tail!

Five Little Astronauts
Five little astronauts
(child holds up fingers of one hand)
Ready for outer space.
The first one said,
(holds up one finger)
"Let's have a race."
The second one said,
(holds up two fingers)
"The weather's too rough."
The third one said,
(holds up three fingers)
"Oh, don't be gruff."
The fourth one said,
(holds up four fingers)
"I'm ready enough."
The fifth one said,
(holds up five fingers)
"Let's blast off!"
10, 9, 8, 7, 6, 5, 4, 3, 2, 1
(starts with ten fingers and puts one down with each number)
BLAST OFF!!
(claps loudly)

Open, Shut Them
(child holds both hands in front of chest)
Open, shut them; open, shut them.
Let your hands go clap.
Open, shut them; open, shut them.
Lay them in your lap.
Walk them, walk them, walk them, walk them.
(makes walking motions up legs and trunk toward head)
Right up to your chin.
Open up your little mouth, but
Do not let them in!
(quickly pulls hands away from chin and hides them behind his back)

Ten Little Indians
(child begins with two hands in front of his chest with all fingers closed)
One little, two little, three little Indians.
(raises left little finger, left ring finger, left middle finger)
Four little, five little, six little Indians.
(raises left forefinger, left thumb, right thumb)
Seven little, eight little, nine little Indians.
(raises right forefinger, right middle finger, right ring finger)
Ten little Indian boys.
(raises right thumb)
Ten little, nine little, eight little Indians.
(closes fingers in reverse)
Seven little, six little, five little Indians.
Four little, three little, two little Indians
One little Indian boy.
(left little finger remains raised)

Five in the Bed
There were five in the bed.
(child holds up five fingers of one hand)
And the little one said,
(wiggles little finger)
Roll over, roll over.
(makes rolling motion from little finger toward thumb, twice)
So they all rolled over,
(rolls hand around in circular motion)
and one fell out
(folds thumb down)
There were four in the bed
(holds up four fingers)
And the little one said,
Roll over, roll over.
So they all rolled over and one fell out
There were three in the bed
(repeats the game)
. . . And one fell out.
There was one in the bed
And the little one said,
Good night, good night.
(folds little finger down)

causing an action by the teacher. The game of "you point and touch, and I say" now moves to the child's own body, with the child providing the initiation and lead in the game while the teacher follows.

The next target behavior is to have the child use words to be the cause of actions by the teacher. The teacher initiates a game in which the child states the name of a body part (knee, chin, etc.) and the teacher points, using her body first and then moving to the child's body. With this accomplished, the child is now using words to be the cause. The child's face should start becoming more animated, with the beginning of a smile and signs of enjoyment.

Step 3: Causal Action Toward Objects

Mirroring is used to begin to establish a bonding process between the difficult child and the teacher. The child gradually comes to enjoy making eye contact with the teacher. The teacher is drawing the child's perceptual awareness outward to recognize outside actions, thus increasing his attention span. The child has learned to cuddle, and now he uses his entire body for a sense of pleasure and comfort as he nestles into the lap of a significant adult. Now the child, just as the infant did during the first year of life, needs to reach out into the world and begin to have an effect on his world (being the cause toward objects). Normally this begins in the infant at age eight to twelve months and dominates toddlers ages twelve to eighteen months. This is typically done by the child's hands through the sense of touch. If touching and extending his hand into the world has been punished, the child will withdraw from touching and panic or flood when the teacher makes such demands.

When most passive children are brought to the finger painting area or water table to enjoy these activities, they appear to panic, refuse to put their hands into the finger paint or other fluids, and wish to flee from the activity. Most aggressive children, on the other hand, are magnetically drawn to such fluid materials; the materials seem to seduce them into stereotypic play, until they lose control (throwing the water aggressively at others or tearing the finger painting paper). It is as if the passive child is dramatically overcontrolled and turned inward (Inside Self), unable to use his hands outwardly with creative materials, while the aggressive child is turned outward (Body Self) and enjoys full use of these materials. The aggressive child's enjoyment, however, is only for the sensory experience and not for creating products, and he is likely to become overwhelmed by these materials. That is why aggressive children are likely to climb into the water table or totally cover themselves with finger paint. In Step 3, Causal Action Toward Objects, the target behavior is to have the child use his hands to actively manipulate materials, first for the sensory pleasure and later to create a product—but always, and especially for the aggressive child, with control.

The teacher sits on a small chair in front of the previously prepared finger paints, with the child on her lap or standing between her legs. For the passive child, the finger paints should be on a very small, cafeteria-type tray (as small as four by six inches); with success, the process will advance to larger and larger trays, eventually to as large as two by three feet. For the aggressive child, the finger painting will occur on a large cafeteria tray, gradually moving to smaller and smaller trays. The tray's raised edges communicate clear boundaries for the child, a message that is not conveyed when finger paints are simply lying on a table. (See the concept of degrees of freedom and control of error in Chapter 6.)

The child is encouraged to experiment by placing his hands into the finger paints and smearing them to enjoy the sensory experience. It is advisable that the child and teacher wear aprons or smocks to protect their clothes from paint. Difficult children can become quite upset if paints get on their clothing, and the apron or smock enables the child to feel much freer in doing such activities. The teacher should experiment with various colors, beginning with light shades (white or yellow) and then moving to more dramatic shades (red, orange, or black). She should make a mental note as to which colors are more upsetting for the child and then make a special effort to introduce these colors gradually.

The most passive and restricted children generally panic at the teacher's first request that they smear paint with their hands. The teacher first models the smearing behavior as a way of introducing the fluid medium to the child. As the teacher holds the child in her lap at the table in front of the finger painting, the teacher brings her arms around the child, places her hands into the paints and begins to smear the paints, covering the entire surface of the tray. The teacher will sing or talk, rocking herself back and forth to give all indications that this is a fun and safe activity.

Next, she manually prompts the child by asking him to place his hands on the back of her hands as she repeats the smearing action. With the child's hands still on the back of hers, she smears with a wooden object such as a pencil, stick, or paintbrush. Next, she drops the object and uses one finger on each hand, and then, finally, she uses her entire hands. The child is now asked to repeat the modeled sequence, first smearing with a wooden object (paintbrush), then one finger on each hand, and finally with full hands. The speed at which the child progresses through this manual prompting will vary greatly, and the teacher must be sensitive to the child's growing anxiety. Over a number of sessions, she must make demands but not rush the child too quickly. Ultimately, the child will reach a point at which he has gained the freedom to engage in fluid painting, and he begins to find joy in the activity. Fluids, especially finger paints, show immediate response to even the most minimal action by the child and give the child the immediate feedback of its sensory feel—the marks with the finger paint show causality.

As they learn to be the cause with objects (finger painting), passive and aggressive children show very different results. The passive child may reject the attempt, requiring the teacher to reinitiate the slowly guided introductory process. The passive child is described as living in an inner world apart from his own body and outside happenings. The fluid medium helps the child to become physically more expressive. The sensory experience with the fluids, which may be initially frightening, is the medium to enable him to become freer and more relaxed and to enjoy such experiences, which are highly attractive to most well-functioning children.

The aggressive child, on the other hand, will only minimally hesitate to engage with such materials. He will tend to dive right in and become more and more active and excited, until the materials begin to take over and he floods, losing control of the materials and himself. He will begin to smear outside the boundaries of the tray, smearing paint up his arms, on nearby tables, or even on the walls. At worst, the child may become aggressive and attempt to smear the teacher and frighten her with the sticky materials. The teacher cannot permit the aggressive child to lose control while finger painting. She brings her hands around the child, placing her hands on top of his and manually and verbally helping him slow down and control the medium. If the loss of control is extremely dramatic, she may have to remove the child from the materials for a short period and then reintroduce him a short time later.

Fluid materials such as finger paints actively permit the teacher to turn the passive child expressively outward, while for the aggressive child—who is already out— finger painting becomes a context for learning control. Once the child has developed the expressive freedom to use such materials freely—but under control within the body world of sensory experience—he will gradually gain the parallel freedom to be expressive in the real world with others.

Once success through finger painting is achieved, the teacher can now present the passive or aggressive child with a full curriculum of fluid play materials (sand play, easel painting, clay, modeling dough, and various drawing materials) to build on the expressive nature of these materials. Soon the child's sensorimotor use of the fluid materials will change to create recognizable symbolic products (instead of merely smearing, the child now paints a picture of a "doggie").

Step 4: Causal Action and the Expression of Ideas and Feelings Through Symbolic Play

It is near the age of two that children begin to show the cognitive capacities to play symbolically. They begin to use toys or even household items to express their fantasy ideas related to their age interest and emotional concerns. (The toddler, for example, uses domestic play themes of "being like mother.") Passive and aggressive young children, possibly ages three to six, may still not demonstrate this ability to express themselves symbolically or ventilate feelings. During Step 4, Symbolic Play, the teacher attempts to reteach the difficult child to play; these first attempts may show strongly aggressive themes.

The teacher brings the child to a rug or floor area with a collection of small miniature toys (micro symbolic toys), such as rubber people, animals, toy furniture, and similar items (see Figure 5.5). She then encourages and asks the child to use these toys in make-believe fantasy play.

Depending on the amount of time the teacher can get free from total classroom supervision, the play facilitation might be done as follows:

1. In a small room, office, or at the end of a hallway
2. During other children's nap period
3. In the block room space, while encouraging similar play with other children under the teacher's supervision
4. While other children are out on the playground

FIGURE 5.5   Suggested Micro Toys

Rubber animal families
Rubber wild animals
Rubber farm animals
A collection of small blocks
Small wooden transportation toys (cars, trucks, and so on)
Miniature playhouse with furniture

The goal of such symbolic fantasy play is to have the child gain the ability to use the world of play and toys to externally express the fears, ideas, and thoughts that reside in his internal world. Initially when the child does play these themes, this play might be full of aggressive content. The teacher may see the child (1) become the aggressor and do unto others as he feels has been wrongly done to him; (2) digest the bad experience piecemeal by replaying themes over and over until he tires and represses it; or (3) change the outcome in fantasy to make it more acceptable.

The teacher's facilitation or intervention to help the child play symbolically will gradually progress up a continuum from an open, noncontrolling position to gradually becoming more closed or controlling. The general techniques, moving from open to closed, are looking, naming, questioning, commanding, and acting. This, of course, is the Teacher Behavioral Continuum (see Chapter 3).

Here is an example of how this process might develop:

Mike is a passive child with whom the teacher has been intervening, using methods found in Steps 1–3, for a number of weeks. She is now attempting to begin techniques in Step 4, Symbolic Play. The teacher and Mike are seated facing each other on the rug in the block section of the classroom, while the remaining children are outside with the classroom aid. Between them are a toy rubber farm and wild animals, small, bendable people, and house furniture.

Mike glances at the toys. He takes a toy tiger, holds it in both hands on his lap, then drops his eyes and takes no other actions.

The teacher looks at Mike and the toys and smiles (looking—nonverbal acknowledgment).

TEACHER (*naming*): "Mike, these are safe toys for you to play with. (commanding) I would like you to take the toys and make any story you would like to make."

Mike reaches out and takes a bendable male doll (a "daddy" toy), now holding the tiger in the right hand and the "daddy" doll in the left hand. The teacher smiles (acknowledgment) and simply looks on for a period of four to six minutes. After a long period of silence and inactivity, Mike brings both of the toys up to his face and appears to visually inspect them.

TEACHER: "Ah, you have a daddy and a tiger." (naming statement as active listening)

Mike takes the male doll and tiger and brings them together in a controlled manner; the teacher can see that the tiger is biting the male doll on the foot. The teacher again smiles (looking as a nonverbal acknowledgment).

Mike's tiger now gently bites the male doll's other foot, then the doll's hand, the other hand, and then its stomach. All of these biting actions are carried out by Mike as if in slow motion, and without any sound or change in his facial expression. Suddenly, the biting becomes vigorous as Mike breaks into a quick smile, and accompanies the tiger's biting action with growling noises. Finally, the tiger bites the male doll's head. Just as suddenly as this intensive biting started, it now stops and Mike places both toys behind him, out of view.

TEACHER: "Ah, the tiger can bite." (naming statements as active listening)

Mike's face becomes expressionless again, and he drops his eyes and becomes inactive. Three to four minutes pass with no action.

TEACHER: "Mike, would you like to tell more of the story?" (question as door opener)

Mike does not respond to the question. He now slides himself over to the small blocks and quite actively builds two uprights with a crosspiece, creating a doorway. This construction is done with the same controlled, slow-motion action. Now Mike places a toy baby lamb in the opening of the blocks and gives a partial smile. Next, all remaining toy animals and people, with the exception of the tiger and daddy behind him, are lined up like a train behind the baby lamb, as if they are in line to pass through the doorway. Mike stops, drops his head, and becomes inactive again for three to four minutes.

TEACHER: "Mike, what will happen next in your story?" ("what" question)

Mike looks for the first time directly at the teacher, making eye contact, and then leans over on his elbows and knees and rapidly builds a full house structure with four walls, using the doorway as the opening to the house. This work is accompanied by many grunting noises from Mike and is done with considerable speech—quite a change from the slow-motion action of all previous activities.

TEACHER: "You have built a house and all the animals and people are waiting to go in." (naming statement as active listening)

Mike now drops his eyes and becomes inactive again for a two-minute period. The teacher simply looks on. Suddenly, Mike reaches behind him, and his right hand appears with the tiger, which advances to the house and the lined-up animals and people. He proceeds to make the tiger crash and destroy the house and lineup. Mike then throws the tiger behind him and across the room, looks intently at the teacher, and again drops his eyes and assumes his previous inactive position.

The teacher waits approximately 30 seconds, then smiles (looking, nonverbal acknowledgment). "Would you like to tell me more of the story?" (question as door opener)

Without looking up, Mike slowly nods his head "yes" but remains inactive.

The teacher now encourages Mike's play to continue, providing nonverbal acknowledgments and asking "what" questions, such as, "What else would happen in your story?" Later, the teacher might tell Mike through a commanding, "Build your house again, and put in furniture," or she may actually pick up the toys and physically intervene and model a make-believe play sequence and theme for Mike. The teacher's play modeling might be putting the people in their beds and having them awaken, eat breakfast, and go off to work. Then the teacher retreats down to commanding and tells the child to "play what I played." If the child is able to carry out this structured play, the teacher moves back along the play facilitation continuum (see Figure 5.6) to more open facilitation through questions: "What is going to happen next?" She then retreats to active listening and acknowledgments. The preferred facilitation method is the open (noncontrolling) technique of simple looking, but if the child does not play, the teacher may advance up and down the continuum (from open to closed, from closed to open) until the child is free to play using his own ideas and initiation.

Generally, a symbolic play facilitation in a one-to-one (teacher-to-child) situation lasts for a period of thirty minutes. The teacher must take the initiative to determine whether the child is tiring and to judge the amount of time to use and how controlling to become. The most effective facilitation requires sessions every day or every other day for a two- to three-week period. But each child is different, and the teacher needs to make a judgment as to how well the symbolic play is progressing. When the child is truly able to play themes with a well-developed story line, the teacher knows he is ready to have other children join him in this fantasy play. The child would finally have reached Step 5, Casual Actions With Coplayers.

The classroom teacher should not attempt to draw conclusions from the projected themes expressed by children in these play sessions. When Mike takes the tiger doll and has it bite the "daddy" doll, the teacher could incorrectly jump to the conclusion that Mike has strong negative feelings toward his father and that some family-child counseling is needed. What is more important is that the child becomes free to do symbolic play. As mentioned earlier, certain themes may appear when the

FIGURE 5.6   Play Facilitation (Teacher Behavioral Continuum)

Open (noncontrolling)				Closed (controlling)
Looking	Naming	Questioning	Commanding	Acting
1. (a). Nonverbal acknowledgment	2. Active listening	1. (b). Door openers 3. "What" questions	4. Tell what to do	5. Teacher plays (models)

child first becomes free to express his strong feelings in play. He may (1) become the aggressor, (2) digest the "bad" experience piecemeal, or (3) change the outcome in fantasy to make it more acceptable. Generally, after one or more of these dimensions of expressing strong feeling is used, the themes move toward more reality-oriented themes, playing out parallel adult roles and behavior.

Becoming Comfortable With Facilitating Fantasy Play

Some teachers, especially those who have been accustomed to direct instruction classrooms and who may have little or no experience closely observing or facilitating young children's fantasy play, may feel uncomfortable with the onlooker role. It is as if the teacher is acting as a "peeping Tom" into the child's personal and emotional world, and she may not know what to expect as the play unfolds. Therefore, it is recommended that teachers new to children's fantasy play read one or more of the classic texts on play facilitation. Axline (1971) is an easy-to-read case study of one child progressing through naming play therapy conducted by the author. Axline (1974) provides many observations and anecdotal descriptions of children's actions during play sessions, with a discussion of procedures for doing such facilitation. Moustakas (1971, 1974) provides many play examples of child behavior and guidelines presented in "how-to" methods. Moustakas (1971) is written directly for the classroom teacher, with some examples of the play of kindergarten children but with a greater focus on older children. Both Axline and Moustakas work from Rogerian theory, a total relationship-listening approach of naming facilitation first developed by Carl Rogers (1969). They give nearly total freedom for the child to begin play, primarily using only looking and active listening, and would probably reject the more controlling techniques of questions, commanding, acting, and modeling. However, difficult children are not viewed here as pathological or emotionally disturbed, and teachers are not doing therapy. Instead, they are teaching and facilitating nonplaying children for them to play, and so more controlling or intrusive techniques are justified.

Step 5: Causal Action With Coplayers

The steps for intervening with passive and aggressive children are based on the idea that the teacher may take the young child through activities paralleling the early stages of development: basic trust with cuddling and modality training (birth to eight months), asserting action toward others (eight to twelve months), asserting actions toward objects, (twelve to eighteen months), and expressing fears and ideas through symbolic play (eighteen months to age three). If this facilitation is successful, the teacher may now begin helping these beginning players learn to express themselves with others as coplayers, a stage normally reached shortly after age three.

To state this clearly, the goal is to have the child learn to be a coplayer by learning to do sociodramatic play. Social behavior by young children includes such actions as waiting in line for their turn and showing social graces by saying "please" and "thank you." But the way the young child becomes truly social is by gaining the ability to act out *scripts* in role play with others.

A three-year-old who stands in an early childhood classroom wearing a man's hat and a woman's skirt and sucking on a toy baby bottle is about to learn to become a role player. This image represents a pivotal time for the child. He is experimenting with a role that he is not (woman's skirt) and the role he will become (man's hat), while still tentatively clinging to the role of infancy (baby bottle) that he must give up.

The make-believe role play as sociodramatic play, playing such roles as mommy, daddy, firefighter, police officer, doctor, and similar roles, enables the child to acquire the give-and-take abilities to coplay with peers that will eventually lead to the ability to become a worker with others (see Figure 5.7).

Sociodramatic play can be defined as including the following elements and characteristics:

1. *Imitative role play*—the child undertakes a make-believe role and expresses it in imitative action and/or verbalization
2. *Make-believe with objects*—toys, unstructured materials, movements, and verbal declarations are substituted for real objects or gestures
3. *Make-believe with actions and situations*—verbal descriptions are substituted for actions and real situations; this consists almost entirely of make-believe, with situations in which the child says, for example, "I'll save you, come back, I'll pick you up"
4. *Persistence in role play*—the child stays with a single role or related role for most of a five-minute time period
5. *Interaction*—at least two players interact within the framework of a socio-dramatic play episode
6. *Verbal communication*—there is some verbal interaction related to a socio-dramatic play episode (Smilansky, 1968)

In Step 5, the facilitation process for the passive or aggressive child, we begin by using the dress-up corner in the regular classroom when the classroom is empty, perhaps when the other children are outdoors. The teacher can bring together the beginning player and two "star" players. The star players are those children who have already demonstrated their ability to engage in elaborate sociodramatic play and would not be threatening to the beginning player. The beginning player and the star

FIGURE 5.7   **Suggested Roles for Sociodramatic Play**

Doctor	Astronaut
Nurse	Pilot
Postal Worker or Letter Carrier	Railway Engineer
Ship's Captain	Cowboy
Bus Driver	Beautician
Electrician	Firefighter
Teacher	Farmer
Police Officer	Restaurant Cook or Waiter
Grocer	Store Attendant

players should have shared a common experience in which they actually observed adults engaged in some form of role activity. This common experience might be one of viewing a film or visiting a post office, police station, fire department, or grocery store—perhaps as part of a class trip. Within a day or two after the shared experience, appropriate props and materials to support role play should be added to the dress-up corner, and the children can be asked to play with the materials and create a make-believe story.

The teacher should partition off the play area so that the children are in close proximity and then seat herself on the periphery of the group to lend her visual support. Initially, there is a "tooling up" period during which the children declare and agree upon their role preferences; the teacher must make sure the beginning player is included. Generally, the ideas should come from the children, and during initial attempts at play it is common for the beginning player to take a subservient role, such as playing the baby or the victim. As subtly and as unobtrusively as possible, the teacher should help the beginning player maintain his role by providing props or even making modeling statements to aid the novice player, who may either forget or be unable to think of what to say. The teacher may continue with many sessions involving these children, and in time add new props, provide new common experiences for roles, and give the beginning player considerable experience with the star players.

If the beginning player is not successful in this first attempt at sociodramatic play, the teacher must demonstrate more structured forms of behavior by modeling (see Figure 5.6). The continuum previously used to facilitate micro play is now used to facilitate sociodramatic play, or macro play. Notice that the teacher first uses the most controlling behaviors of modeling but gradually moves across the continuum to more open techniques.

The teacher may ask the beginning player to watch as she "plays" with the star players. After they carry out a short sequence of sociodramatic play, the exact sequence can be replayed or expanded with the beginning player taking over the modeled part that the teacher played, while the teacher provides both visual and verbal prompting support. The teacher may continue to support the play of the beginning player with commands ("Lie down and pretend that you are a sleeping firefighter, and when the alarm rings, jump up and put on your hat and get on the fire engine") and then move to the less controlling questions ("What will happen to the injured man?"). The teacher may then move to naming statements ("I see that all the firefighters are now on the fire engine ready to leave"), finally retreating to a position of looking as a nonparticipating observer.

The teacher may now ask the three children to make up their own story; when the beginning player carries this out with increased participation and performance, the teacher can become more open in the use of the techniques on the play facilitation continuum, moving to naming statements and looking. As the teacher finds more classroom time to facilitate the play of the beginning player in sociodramatic play during normal classroom play times, these individualized sessions will be needed less frequently. With the attainment of the ability to engage in sociodramatic play, the previously difficult child will become a well-integrated member of the class and a productive player to the fullest extent of his abilities.

Catch Them Being Good

The directive to "catch them being good" is often given by the behaviorist, which suggests that the teacher needs to be attentive to the difficult child's positive and desired behaviors and actions and then to praise or positively reinforce them with primary reinforcers, such as food or tokens that can be collected and turned in for treats, and social reinforcers, such as attention, touch, or verbal praise from the teacher. If teachers reinforce these positive behaviors, the behaviors will be maintained and repeated.

The daily guidance program described here requires the teacher to observe the passive or aggressive child hourly for a two-week period, watching for positive and cooperative behaviors by the child. However, the justification for the teacher's physical and verbal mirroring is quite different from the behaviorist's use of praise, rewards, and reinforcers.

The behavior of difficult children in the classroom ranges from helpless passivity to defensive aggressiveness, with a life stance based on their reasoning that they are powerless. These difficult children have unknowingly convinced themselves that their actions cannot be the cause in the world and enable them to make their world meet their needs. They may not even know what their wants and needs are, and they regress to behaviors that are nonproductive for the passive child and destructive for the aggressive child.

To guide these children toward more productive behaviors, the teacher should use these strategies daily for a two- to three-week period, observing hourly the difficult child and watching for any self-initiating actions. Krown (1969) describes an example of the minimum assertive self-initiative actions:

> . . . dull and sporadic. It consisted largely of holding objects such as dolls, cars, and driving wheels, while, presumably, some internal fantasy with these objects was taking place. Occasionally, the objects would stimulate the children to some short-lived activity such as making automobile noises, wrapping the doll in a blanket, arranging the dishes, and piling some blocks. There seemed to be fleeting concentration and much moving from one piece of equipment to another. (Krown, 1969, p. 59)

This "making automobile noises, wrapping the doll in a blanket, arranging the dishes, and piling some blocks" is just what to look for to "catch them being good." These minimal seeds of play need to be nurtured by the teacher to develop in the child full play ability and full causality.

Applying the Teacher Behavioral Continuum

Earlier chapters use the teacher behaviors on the Teacher Behavioral Continuum (TBC) to guide the child away from negative behaviors (fighting over a toy, using a paintbrush as a sword, or throwing sand), but the same teacher behaviors of looking, naming, and questioning are used to support positively initiated behaviors by the difficult children.

Larry, seated with his legs under him on the rug in the block corner, has selected a small toy automobile. He bends over and, taking one hand, pushes the automobile back and forth three times, making automobile noises. This is an open playtime, and the teacher is supervising a large part of the classroom, but she sees this minimal causal action of Larry's and knows that this is a teachable moment for her. She takes a small similar automobile from the shelf, establishes eye contact with Larry, and makes the same imitative actions of car noises and pushing back and forth—she motorically mirrors his activity. The teacher is physically twenty feet (proxemics-far) away from Larry. Larry looks at the teacher, gives her a slight smile of recognition, and puts the car again on the floor. He gives the car one push, makes no noises, and returns it to his lap. Now he watches the teacher. The teacher mirrors his actions—one push and no sound. In the next three to five minutes Larry initiates more and more elaborate play with the automobile, with the teacher mirroring his activities.

What is the teacher doing? The young infant as a lap baby makes a sound, burps, or moves his arms with joy, and the mother imitates and mirrors the infant's actions. The child gives a smile of recognition to the mother and repeats the action. The mother follows for the second time. This ballet of actions, in which the infant initiates and mother follows, helps the infant learn to be the cause of actions in the world and learn to feel powerful.

"Catching them being good" begins a similar ballet of actions between the passive or aggressive child and the teacher, as she attempts to help him develop a sense of causality through play. According to Parten's social stages (see Figure 2.1), the teacher is performing parallel play with Larry. Over many days, the teacher will spend only three to six minutes mirroring Larry's activities. Over time she moves within three feet of Larry (proxemics-near) and gives him other toy props (associative play), such as blocks for building streets and a garage for his automobile. Finally, other children see this activity and send signals that they wish to join the automobile play. Now Larry can move into associative play. The teacher has accomplished this transition through the TBC's looking and mirroring motorically his activities, but at this point she has not spoken or been verbally directive in any manner.

The daily campaign for motor mirroring should and can be done in a host of actions that last only seconds. Larry yawns; the teacher does the same. Larry and the teacher exchange a smile of recognition. At lunch, Larry's pea rolls off his spoon; the teacher imitates the same, making eye contact, and the smile is exchanged. The teacher mirrors any normal, nonaggressive action, play or nonplay, during the day, possibly during arrivals, circle time, washing hands, in the playground, or at departure time. For a two- to four-week period, Larry is periodically bathed in mirroring activity, which is done in a light, humorous, and fun manner.

For the passive child who lives in the Inside Self, this motoric mirroring by the teacher breaks through the child's self-imposed isolation and causes the child to gain an understanding of the outside world and his effect on it. For the passive child, this will take much time. The aggressive child, who lives in the Body Self, will join quickly in this play mirroring. The teacher may even face the problem that the child will get too excited and carry this parallel to an extreme. The teacher will then need to channel this excitement *from the body to the toy, from the toy to play, and from play to work* (see Figure 4.4).

Once an infant has begun to get a sense of causality, he moves as a toddler to "Mommy, do for me" (Mahler et al., 1975). He repetitively brings objects to mother's hands and looks on (Parten, 1933). The mother then takes the object, verbally encodes (names) it, and motorically shows its meaning (Piaget, 1951). "Larry, cars go (pushes back and forth making car noises) var-oom, varr-oom." The toddler brings boxes to be opened, car keys, the dog's water bowl, and just about anything for the mother to name. Similarly, the teacher may begin naming objects with the difficult child who is now beginning to play, while actively listening (Gordon, 1974; 1988). "Oh, Larry, I see that you have made a road with blocks and a little small garage for your car to have its own house." The teacher uses naming and active listening all day long when she finds the difficult child "being good," that is, initiating any ideas that are not aggressive or passive. Through this naming, the child gains a self-awareness of his actions and his impact on the world.

In a daily campaign to have the child actively engaged in classroom activities, the teacher may also move to the TBC's questioning. Questions during the "catch them being good" campaign should not be to have the child answer questions in regard to facts, labeling, and explanations, but to encourage him to be reflective and to facilitate his own motor activities or play. "Larry, where do you think you could hang your coat this morning? Larry, what could you say to Walter to have him pass you the basket of cookies? Larry, what could you do with the napkin after you are done eating?"

Finally, after much growth on Larry's part, the teacher may begin to use commands or acting by intervening and teaching specific things through modeling. Commands and acting should only be used after the difficult child has moved to associative activities (Parten, 1933).

Summary

Facilitation with aggressive or passive children generally is a process of one-to-one play with children who are stalled in their social-emotional development. The steps of this facilitation process bring together many of the techniques and theoretical constructs developed in the first three chapters of this book. The teacher needs to understand the passive and aggressive constructs on which children will respond to life's demands and frustrations by moving from passivity to physical aggression, verbal aggression, and then to expressive language. This chapter suggests a view of the problem child as one who is stalled in one of these passive or aggressive life stances, and the intervention process will help facilitate the child's development.

The teacher carries out that facilitation by working to get the child to bond with her, to learn to be the cause toward others, to learn to express his inner tensions through fluids and symbolic play, and, finally, to use expressive language—become a coplayer with other children. Central to this intervention is the value of play as a process essential to normal growth and development. When the child cannot play, his energy is either turned inward as passivity or outward as aggression. The goal is to turn out the passive child and channel the aggressive child through the construct of the body to the toy, the toy to play, and play to working with others. It is when the child can attain sociodramatic play that he has reached the high level of functioning socialization desired in these early years. With the ability to do sociodramatic play, the child now becomes fully adaptive. The teacher should now have a well-functioning child who exhibits little or no passivity and physical or verbal aggression. (Note: Like any behavior, the ability to perform sociodramatic play will be affected by tiredness, health, and similar factors.)

REFERENCES

Alberto, P. A. and Troutman, A. C. (1990) *Applied behavior analysis for teachers* (3rd ed.). New York: Merrill-Macmillan.

Axline, V. M. (1971). *Dibs: In search of self.* New York: Ballantine Books.

Axline, V. M. (1974). *Play therapy* (6th ed.). New York: Ballantine Books.

Elkisch, P. (1957). Psychological significance of mirror. *Journal of American Psychoanalytical Association, 5,* 235–244.

Erikson, E. (1950). *Childhood and society.* New York: W. W. Norton.

Freud, A. (1968). *Normality and pathology in childhood: Assessment of development.* New York: International Universities Press.

Gordon, T. (1974). *T.E.T.: Teacher effectiveness training.* New York: David McKay.

Gordon, T. (1988). *Teaching children self-discipline: At home and at school.* New York: Times Books.

Harris, T. A. (1969). *I'm ok—you're ok: A practical guide to transactional analysis.* New York: Harper & Row.

Krown, S. (1974). *Threes and fours go to school.* Upper Saddle River, NJ: Prentice Hall.

Mahler, M. S. (1970). *On human symbiosis and the vicissitudes of individuation.* New York: International Universities Press.

Mahler, M. S., Pine, S., & Bergman, A. (1975). *The psychological birth of the human infant.* New York: Basic Books.

Moustakas, C. (1971). *The authentic teacher: Sensitivity and awareness in the classroom.* Cambridge, MA: Howard A. Doyle.

Moustakas, C. (1974). *Psychotherapy with children: The live relationship.* New York: Ballantine Books.

Parten, M . (1933). Social play among preschool children. *Journal of Abnormal and Social Psychology, 28,* 136–147.

Piaget, J. (1951). *Play, dreams, and imitation in childhood.* New York: W. W. Norton.

Rogers, C. (1969). *Freedom to learn.* Columbus, OH: Charles E. Merrill.

Smilansky, S. (1968). *The effects of sociodramatic play on disadvantaged preschool children.* New York: John Wiley and Sons.

Winnicott, D. (1971). *Playing and reality.* London: Travistock Publications.

Wolfgang, C. H., Mackender, B., & Wolfgang, M. E. (1981). *Growing and learning through play.* Paoli, PA: Judy/Instructo.

Wolfgang, C. H., & Wolfgang, M. E. (1992) *School for young children: Developmentally appropriate practices.* Boston: Allyn and Bacon.

SUGGESTED READING

Smilansky, S., & Shefatya, L. (1990). *Facilitating play: A medium for promoting cognitive, socio-emotional and academic development in young children.* Gaithersburg, MD: Psychosocial & Educational Publications.

6 Teaching Young Children to Play

Mike is seated before a puzzle, and he appears to have drifted off into some internal fantasy (Inside Self), unable to complete the puzzle before him and unaware that other play activities are going on around him. Alicia is not able to place her hands into the finger paint and rejects all things "messy," refusing also to use paint or draw (not able to use Body Self). Finally, Marsha is pulled into the dramatic play of more bossy children who give her the role of the baby, which requires her to do little role play and uses little to no language or enactment with objects to do any real fantasy play (not able to use the Social Self).

How does the teacher guide these children into such play? The answer is that she must consider two structures to create an intervention and facilitation process: the degrees of freedom inherent in constructed and various play materials, and the degrees of freedom the teacher uses by her own behavior related to the actions on the Teacher Behaviorial Continuum (TBC): looking, naming, questioning, commanding, and acting.

The Structure of Play Materials

There are generally five types of play and play materials used in the classroom:

Construction (producing symbolic products)

1. Fluid construction (water play, dry sand, easel painting, clay, and drawing)
2. Structured construction (unit blocks, Legos, Montessori [1965] materials, and puzzles)

Symbolic play (fantasy or make-believe play)

3. Dramatic play, done with micro toys (small representation of people, animals, furniture, etc.)
4. Sociodramatic play done with macro toys and materials (child-size furniture and dress-up props)

Sensorimotor Play

5. Body practice (Gerhardt, 1973).

Construction (Fluid vs. Structured)

For the materials, most commonly called art materials, that are used in the classroom to make products, a number of Piagetian insights can be applied to give a deeper understanding.

Centeredness and Irreversibility.   Piaget (1965) demonstrated that dynamic fluid materials (water play, finger painting, clay, and so on) can present an intellectual challenge for two- to seven-year-olds who are in the stage of preoperational thinking (Brearley, 1969). The young child's thinking is described as centered and irreversible, and he is incapable of comprehending movement between states.

To demonstrate the centeredness of a child's thinking, Piaget presented two equal quantities of clay in the form of two clay balls to a child. After the child agreed that the two balls were equal in volume, Piaget, as the child was watching, rolled one ball into a sausage shape. Piaget found that the preschool-age child would either declare that now the sausage had more clay "because it is longer" or that the ball had more clay because "it is higher." A young child centers intuitively on the one visual dimension, either length or height. Unlike adults with higher-order thinking, the young child cannot simply mentally reverse the sequence of events to realize that nothing was added or taken away and, therefore, that the two portions of clay must still be equal. The irreversibility of thought limits the child's understanding of volume, time, space, causality, and the use of fluid materials.

States vs. Transformations.   To explore children's ways of thinking related to transformation, Piaget presented a child with a pencil held in a vertical position above a tabletop. The pencil was permitted to fall to rest on the table in a horizontal position. The child was then asked to draw a picture of the movement of the pencil. Of the many children tested, at various ages, the preschoolers represented the pencil in the static vertical state and the static horizontal state, but it was not until the early elementary ages that children demonstrated an understanding of the transformation (movement) between states and drew the pencil in various descending stages. This inability to comprehend transformations is a characteristic of the young child and becomes particularly apparent when he is required to understand any dynamic change in his world. For example, a child younger than age seven, the preoperational child, has difficulty understanding the children's story of the Ugly Duckling (in which the ugly ducking is transformed into a beautiful swan). Similarly, young children have difficulty understanding tadpoles transforming into frogs, seeds transforming into plants, eggs transforming into baby chicks, and so on (Brearley, 1969).

The use of fluids, such as finger paints, water play, or even pouring juice at snack time by a young child, presents a major intellectual challenge. For a child to simply pour water from a larger container to a receiving container would involve a classic example of a transformation (change in states). For the child to understand when to stop pouring requires decentering (taking into consideration at least two variables) and coordinating the two containers and the flow of the water.

Fluid materials also are heavily involved in early prohibitions and moral training in the very young child (toddlerhood), and spills and messiness bring quick and emotional intervention by supervising and caring adults (Piaget, 1965). These fluid materials, therefore, evoke for many children feelings of shame and doubt about their own abilities to use and touch them, especially if these early experiences brought harsh punishment or reprimands (Erikson, 1950). These abundant and common fluid materials present both an intellectual and emotional challenge to the very young child, which is why some children reject the use of water play, painting, and clay materials.

Degrees of Freedom and Control of Error

To help the child become comfortable with such fluid materials, two new concepts can help teachers understand construction materials: *degrees of freedom* and *control of error*. Consider this hypothetical water play on an outside playground. A galvanized water tank, the kind normally used for watering lambs on a farm or ranch, is solidly anchored to the ground and sits in a boxed-in bed of gravel to permit quick drainage of water that spills to the ground. The tank, six feet long by two feet wide and fifteen inches deep, is filled with ten inches of soapy water. It also contains hoses, siphons, pouring devices, and a collection of miniature rubber real-life toys, including boats and similar sailing vessels. On hot summer days, the children wear bathing suits to water play.

Contrast this outdoor water play with indoor water play in a typical Montessori (1965) classroom. One child has picked up an oval-shaped metal tray (twelve inches by six inches) from the shelf on which it was stored. The child takes the tray—which is designed to be used by only one child—and carries it by its two handles to a small child-size table and chair. The child seats herself and begins to remove items from the tray. First she opens a paper towel and places it on the table in front of her. Next, she takes a small porcelain bathroom soap dish containing a small sponge and puts it next to the hand towel. One at a time, the child removes two small pitchers (like those seen for oil and vinegar at a restaurant salad bar), using the handles of each to place them facing each other on the towel. One pitcher is empty, and the second is filled with water colored with blue food dye. The child now water plays by pouring the blue water from one container to the other and back again without spilling. If some water is spilled, the child wipes it up with the small sponge. Once the child has finished with the activity, the items are placed back on the tray, the tray is returned to the shelf, and the wet paper towel is thrown in the trash.

Obviously, these are two dramatically different forms of water play with regard to openness for free expression of the child's behavior and demands for control. *Degrees of freedom* is a concept that describes the degree to which children may take play materials and use them in any creative manner they wish. The large outdoor water tub has maximum degrees of freedom, permitting children the widest range of use for expression of their ideas and wishes. The Montessori (1965) water pouring has minimum degrees of freedom, and the child must perform the motor meanings or motor actions dictated by how the materials were engineered and how the teacher has instructed that they should be used. Therefore, the Montessori water play is said to be structured.

An understanding of the degrees of freedom concept regarding materials allows the teacher to evaluate all the play materials that are normally placed in a construction play–based classroom. These materials traverse a continuum that arranges materials from maximum to minimum degrees of freedom, beginning with water play, dry sand, and finger painting and advancing to easel painting, clay, drawing (with any items), blocks, Legos, Montessori (1965) equipment, puzzles, Lotto-type games, and finally, the computer (see Figure 6.1).

The maximum to minimum degrees of freedom construct regarding materials enables the teacher to design a well-balanced classroom and a balanced play environment. These materials can be used for structured construction and fluid construction types of play, as well as make-believe symbolic micro play and macro play. This design also enables the teacher to assess the effect on the behavior of the highly active, aggressive (or introverted, passive) child who is placed with fluid construction materials that offer maximum degrees of freedom (such as the large outdoor water tank) or with structured construction materials that offer minimum degrees of freedom (puzzles). Chapter 5 demonstrated how the teacher can deliberately use various materials, with their innate degrees of freedom, for purposes of intervening and facilitating the play of difficult children.

Now consider this scenario: A group of three three-year-olds is using magic markers on a circular table. When one of the markers rolls off and under the table, two of the children crawl under the table to retrieve the lost marker. The third child accidentally steps on one child's fingers, while the second hits his head on the underside of the table and begins to cry.

The magic markers and the way they were laid out and organized was the root of this difficulty. The teacher can change the organization of the materials and how they are arranged to eliminate such difficulties. Such deliberate engineering on the teacher's part is called *control of error*.

Now consider another classroom, where the teacher has taken the markers and cemented (using plaster of Paris) the marker caps upside down in an empty, cleaned tuna can. The markers can now be placed back into the cemented caps and placed on the table for the children to use, providing a number of benefits. The children may take out, use, and replace the markers, always knowing where they belong. In addition, storing the markers in fixed caps prevents them from rolling off the table, and since the markers are now stored facing down, gravity will keep the tips wet for quick use by the child. There is now less likelihood that the markers would be lying about on a table or in a box, accidentally marking the table or drying out in the open air

FIGURE 6.1   Play Materials Continuum

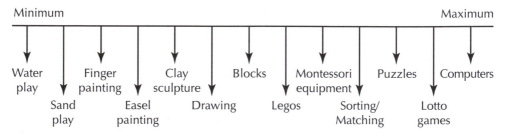

and rolling off the table. The teacher has deliberately engineered into the activity and materials control of error. Thus, a child is less likely to make a mistake or have a problem using the material, and the teacher has eliminated some potential discipline problems, such as having children scrambling on hands and knees under the table and across the floor chasing a runaway marker.

The big outdoor tank for water play described earlier offered a great degree of freedom, but it also was engineered with much thought regarding control of error. Since it was (1) placed outdoors, (2) placed in a boxed-in surface with gravel to control water runoff, and (3) the children were in bathing suits, there was only a minimal possibility that the teacher would need to intervene to stop or control some action or error made by the children during water play.

Teachers much evaluate every space and all materials to determine if they can creatively engineer these items, using the concept of control of error, so that children may be free to use materials with little concern for breakage or for the kinds of accidents that may disrupt daily classroom activities. Puzzles that have many pieces that tend to get lost can be stored and used on small cafeteria trays. Legos, with their greater expense and number of pieces to control, may be used on a larger cafeteria tray, or a Lego table can be purchased to help confine the pieces and make them easier to control. Smocks for painting, plastic eye shields for hammering at the carpentry table, mouth guards for the water fountain to prevent children from sucking on the outlet—all these features provide *control of error*.

The materials continuum (see Figure 6.1) displays construction materials from fluid to structured. The fluid materials on the most open end of the continuum lack any structure, taking the form of the containers in which they are placed (water play). More structured materials begin to maintain their shape (painting, clay, and pencils for drawing), but these materials still grant the child maximum degrees of freedom to express his own ideals with the materials. Adding water to dry sand, making it clay-like, also makes it more structured.

Materials such as unit blocks maintain their shape and form but still can be used, given the characteristic of the materials, to make their own products. Finally, moving to the closed end of the materials continuum, puzzles, Montessori equipment, and even computers are considered structured and lack the degrees of freedom.

Teachers can use this understanding of the degree of structure embedded in materials to guide and intervene with the nonplaying child. Generally, the passive child rejects the fluid materials, unable to enjoy simple sensory experiences or to produce recognizable symbols and products. The aggressive child, however, will actively jump into these fluids but will become so excited with the use of the fluid activity that he will lose control and begin to use the materials destructively.

Teaching Children to Use Fluid Construction

Water play: When using all materials, both fluid and structured construction, the goal is to have the children use the materials in an expressive manner, but with control. Generally, children respond in one of three ways when invited to play with water and similar fluids. Some are comfortable and enjoy it immensely. Others reject the materials completely. The third group begins tentative play with water and then gradually increases the tempo until they are splashing and throwing water or actually climbing into the container—the materials seem to take over.

Again, the two structures for helping children become effective with fluids such as water play are (1) the degrees of freedom inherent in various play materials and (2) the degrees of freedom the teacher grants using the Teacher Behaviorial Continuum (TBC).

The child who rejects water play may be directed to the Montessori method described earlier. The Montessori water play has maximum control of error, and the child can have early success with pouring so that he becomes comfortable with the materials. The next step is to move the child to a small plastic tub, possibly containing only one inch of water, and provide miniature toys, tubes, and plastic hoses. Later, the teacher may add liquid soap, thus providing more degrees of freedom. When the child has mastered this medium, he would move to a stand-up water table (less control of error) and then finally to a large water play area such as the outdoor tank previously described (minimum control of error). Simply by designing the equipment and water play materials, the teacher starts with a structured, closed-end design with maximum control of error and then gradually moves along a continuum with these same water play media, enabling the child to use minimum control of error and maximum degree of freedom. This is exactly the procedure demonstrated in the intervention process (see Chapter 5). The teacher is engineering the degrees of openness of the materials to have the overly controlled, passive children become more and more expressive.

The teacher accompanies the presentation of the various forms of water play with teacher action from the TBC (looking, naming, questioning, commanding, and acting).

The teacher places the Montessori containers (acting) on the tray before the child. The teacher takes from the tray and places before her on the table the sponge, paper towel, and the two pitchers. She models pouring from one pitcher to the other, returns the pitchers to the tray, wipes up with the sponge, and then dries off the table with the paper towel.

> TEACHER (*commanding*): "Angela, you play as I played. Pick this up and put it on the table." (pointing) The teacher moves the tray in front of the child.
>
> TEACHER (*questioning*): "How could you pour the blue water into this container?"
>
> TEACHER (*naming*): "Oh, I see you have put all of the things on the table, and you are pouring."

The teacher has been working with the child at proxemics-intimate (looking). Now she moves her chair back (proxemics-near), and then departs (proxemics-far), permitting the child to practice pouring on her own.

In this example, the teacher began with maximum control by starting with the TBC's acting; thus the child had minimum degrees of freedom. Gradually moving across the TBC, the teacher granted the child much freer use of the materials. The teacher could have moved in the opposite direction if Angela initiated activity by just looking or looking and naming, thus granting the child maximum degrees of freedom. Again, once the child is comfortable in doing this structured Montessori water play, the child would move to the tub with one inch of water, the standing water table, and so on, and the teacher would guide the water play using the TBC.

The above guidance with Angela was based on the idea that she rejected the materials, much as a passive child might do. An aggressive child who could not use the large outdoor water tank with control could be moved to the standing water table, then to the tub with one inch of water, and finally, if need be, to the Montessori tray where he is monitored and facilitated by the teacher's actions (TBC).

Finger painting (or dry sand): The same process of control of error can be done with finger painting as was done with the water play. The continuum with finger painting would be as follows (most structured to least):

1. A small cafeteria tray or a pie pan with raised edges used for serving coffee or tea—the raised edges define clearly the boundaries
2. A normal size cafeteria tray (ten by twelve inches)
3. A very large tray (two by three feet)
4. Finger painting on paper at a small open table
5. Finger painting at a large open table

The raised edges on the trays clearly define the boundaries for the aggressive child, while the passive child is encouraged by the teacher to fill up all the space. The teacher intervenes to help the aggressive child physically control his hands, while she facilitates the passive child by having him place his hands on top of hers, thus feeling the free movement as she finger paints.

Easel painting: The structure of easel painting using degrees of freedom might move from most controlled to least as follows:

1. Paint within a paper picnic plate, using a large paintbrush (the aggressive child needs to stay inside the edges and boundaries of the plate, while the passive child needs to cover all the paper plate space with paint).
2. A fresh paper plate is tacked (or taped) to the easel, and the child uses it as a target (the aggressive child stays inside of the plate, and the passive child fills up the plate space).
3. The plate is taken away, and the child can paint on white paper the same size as the plate (six inches).
4. The passive child paints on paper twelve by twelve inches; the aggressive child paints on large full sheets of painting paper.
5. The passive child paints on a full sheet of painting paper; the aggressive child paints on a smaller sheet of paper (twelve by twelve inches) and then on a paper plate pinned to the easel surface.

Again, the teacher uses the TBC to guide the child in these painting activities:

The teacher (looking) places her hand lightly on the child's shoulder.

   TEACHER (*naming*): "Paints are exciting and sometimes hard to control."

   TEACHER (*questioning*): "Where does the paint go?"

   TEACHER (*commanding*): "Keep the paint inside the paper plate."

The teacher (acting) brings her hand gently over the child's hand and slows him down physically.

Drawing with pencils, crayons, magic markers, or chalk could be structured in a similar manner. See Figure 6.2 for the developmental stages of painting, drawing, and most flat artwork.

Unit Blocks (or Legos): Blocks, which maintain their shape and form but are *not* engineered to produce one product, are safe media for both aggressive and passive children. The passive child may be frightened by the possibility of building high towers and then having them fall down or get knocked down and will mainly build flat, enclosed structures that hug the floor. The aggressive child will want to stack and knock down the blocks. The teacher could make a rule that children should build as high as their belt but then take blocks down rather than knocking them down. Using the TBC the teacher can guide this play.

The developmental stages of block building are as follows:

1. Blocks are carried around but not used for construction
2. Building begins; children make mostly rows, either horizontal (on the floor) or vertical (stacking), with much repetition
3. Bridging—two blocks with a space between, connected by a third space
4. Enclosures—blocks placed in such a way that they enclose space
5. When facility with blocks is acquired, decorative patterns appear; much symmetry can be observed
6. Naming of structures for dramatic play begins; before this stage, children may also have named their structures, but the names were not necessarily related to the function of their building
7. Children's buildings often reproduce or symbolize actual structures they know, and there is a strong impulse toward dramatic play around the block structures (Hirsch, 1974)

Block play, done with large quantities of blocks on an open floor space with micro toys (miniature life), is ideal for facilitating the social stages (unoccupied, solitary, onlooker, parallel, associative, and cooperative—see Figure 2.1). The teacher can use the TBC to guide and support this social play.

Puzzles and similar structured items: Puzzles, as true structured construction materials, have built within them varied degrees of structure related to difficulty. A four-piece puzzle is easier than a six-piece puzzle, and then when more pieces are added the puzzles become more difficult. Also, the symbol or picture on the puzzle can be simple or complex, providing varying degrees of prompts or cues to the child that help him figure out how to place and solve the puzzle. The teacher can

FIGURE 6.2   Developmental Stages of Drawing

 1–2 years: random scribbling. The child uses random scribble marks simply as a sensorimotor activity.

 2–2½ years: controlled scribbling. The child begins to develop some control of his fine motor abilities, and the scribbles gain some direction and control. After some experience with controlled scribbling, a child may name his picture a "motorcycle" or a "big wheel," although there appears to be no resemblance. This is an intellectual accomplishment for the child, an indication that he is taking his first step toward being able to do representation.

 2½–3 years: the face. The next major development is for the circle to become a face.

 3½–4 years: arms and legs. The circle "person" develops stick arms and legs, which protrude from the circle, or the head; there is no body yet.

 4 years: the body. The human figure begins to acquire a body. Gradually, more and more body parts are added (hands, feet, hair, ears, etc.).

 5 years: the floating house. First "house" drawings usually resemble a face, with windows placed like eyes and door like a mouth. These first houses are usually somewhere in the middle of the paper and seem to be floating in space.

 5½–6 years: the house on a bottom line. The bottom of the paper is used as a baseline and the house rests on it.

 5½–6 years: a baseline supports the house. A base line appears within the drawing and the house rests on it.

 6–7 years: two-dimensional drawing. The baseline begins to take on the quality of a horizon, which indicates the child's awareness of two-dimensional space.

experiment with a collection of forty to sixty puzzles in the classroom by watching effective players use the puzzles. Gradually the teacher will be able to classify the puzzles into five groups of increasing difficulty and to label them with small pieces of colored tape to indicate the level of difficulty for each puzzle.

Puzzles, as they become more complex, will be very taxing and demanding for both the passive and the aggressive child. Passive children seat themselves before the puzzles and tend to drift off into space. The teacher will need to use the structure of her own guidance to facilitate puzzles play—again, the TBC steps.

> The teacher (looking) finds Mike seated before a puzzle, and he appears to have drifted off into some internal fantasy (Inside Self), unable to complete the puzzle before him and unaware that other play activities are going on around him. The teacher moves to proxemics-near (taking a seat next to him), and looks at Mike's face and back to the puzzle.
>
> TEACHER (*naming*): "Puzzles are sometimes hard to do! I see you have a puzzle piece with the dog's eye on it, and you are looking for another piece with a second eye to match it."
>
> TEACHER (*questioning*): "What do you see on this piece?"
>
> MIKE: "The doggie's nose."
>
> TEACHER (*questioning*): "What do you see on this piece?"
>
> MIKE: "The doggie's mouth."
>
> TEACHER (*questioning*): "Could you put these two pieces together?"
>
> TEACHER (*commanding*): "Pick up this piece with an ear, and try it here, here, or here, to see if it will fit in one of these spots."

The teacher (acting) picks up a piece and adds it to the puzzle to get Mike started. If Mike continues to drift off into his dream world, the teacher pulls up a movable mirror and uses the mirroring technique described in Chapter 5 (Elkisch, 1957). She plays with him, and once he appears to initiate activity (being the cause through the mirroring play), Mike is brought back quickly to the puzzle to see if he can "be the cause" with the puzzle.

Similar Montessori structured items, interlocking shapes, form boards, Lotto games, and computers would be facilitated with teacher guidance.

Facilitating and Guiding Symbolic Play

The goal is to have the child use micro toys (small representations of people, animals, furniture, etc.) to play out make-believe or fantasy play (Anker, Jones, and Willison, 1974). When doing dramatic play at its most developed level, the child would make the toy items imitate a role, sustain the theme of the play for many minutes, and use gestures, objects, or representations of imaginary objects and people to produce some form of drama and events. Play with miniature toys does not easily support cooperative play, and when this does occur it is usually between two children who are very good friends and often play together. Again, the teacher would facilitate this play with the TBC.

> The beginning player has pulled out a basket with miniature-life farm animals, with small blocks nearby. The teacher (looking) pulls over a small chair, makes eye contact with the child, and smiles to encourage the use of these items.
>
> **TEACHER** (*naming*): "Oh, I see that you have a cow, a sheep, and a chicken."
>
> **TEACHER** (*questioning*): "What could the cow do? What fun things could happen in your story with these animals?"
>
> **TEACHER** (*commanding*): "Pick out some small blocks and make a corral for your horses." After no productive play by the beginning player the teacher states, "Watch me, and see the story that I can make."
>
> The teacher (acting) takes the miniature toys, makes a barn, and corral, and plays out a theme of farm animals for a five-minute period.

In the following example, the teacher moves back down the TBC, attempting to grant the child autonomy.

> **TEACHER** (*commanding*): "You play what I played."
>
> **TEACHER** (*questioning*): "What else could happen in your story?"
>
> **TEACHER** (*naming*): "Oh, I see the cows are eating grass, and the chickens are laying eggs."
>
> Finally, the teacher simply looks on (proxemics-near) and leaves the area with the child continuing to play without the teacher's visual support.

Sociodramatic play done with macro toys and materials (child-size furniture and dress-props) is considered to be the demonstration of the most sophisticated play form during the ages three to seven (Curry, 1974). Characteristic of the aggressive and passive preschoolers is their difficulty in engaging in such social play, the skill necessary for them to become effective socially. To engage in sociodramatic play, the child must have passed through the social stages of unoccupied, solitary, parallel, onlooker, associative, and cooperative play (Parten, 1971). Once the passive and aggressive child can play sociodramatically, the negative behaviors of passivity and aggression disappear because of his newfound ability to symbolically represent his ideas and communicate his needs, both through language and nonverbally, thus enabling him to be a cooperative worker with others (Brissett & Edgley, 1975; Freud, 1971).

The behaviors the teacher is attempting to teach in sociodramatic play are (1) to enact or imitate a role, (2) to sustain the theme for ten minutes or more, (3) to use gestures and objects to represent imaginary objects or people, (4) to interact with a second child or more, and (5) to have a verbal exchange.

A beginning player, Jimmy, stands as an onlooker at the end of the housekeeping area watching two other children pretending to be mommy and daddy as they set the table, cook at the stove, and place their baby (a doll) in a small high chair. The teacher's goal is to help Jimmy get into this play and demonstrate the five behaviors in sociodramatic play. The TBC is used again to guide and facilitate this play (see Figure 6.3).

FIGURE 6.3   The TBC: Facilitation of Sociodramatic Play

Looking	Naming	Questioning	Commanding	Acting
The teacher supportively looks on (proxemics-near) to encourage Jimmy to play out a variety of fantasies that might potentially be frightening—the teacher stands by to assist those children who get overexcited or lost in an aggressive fantasy.	The teacher verbally mirrors the beginning play actions of the child. (Example: "I see you have the dishes and are ready to set the table.")	The teacher uses questions to encourage children to play out and further develop fantasy themes. (Example: "Now that the table is set, what's going to happen next?")	The teacher helps the children select, start, or further develop their play themes by directly assigning roles ("You're the mommy. You're the doctor.") or by directly describing a new development in their play theme. (Example: "Now that you've finished setting the table, the doorbell rings and the mail carrier has a special delivery letter.")	The teacher introduces a new prop to encourage further play or assumes a part and inserts herself into the play. (Example: The teacher picks up the telephone and calls the doctor.)

Summary

The teacher has two structures to use in guiding and facilitating young children in play—the varying degrees of the structure of objects and materials (fluid to structured) and the structure of the teacher's own behaviors and actions (the TBC). The object is to have children learn to control and be expressive with these materials and then begin to produce recognizable symbols in their products in construction and to enact fantasy roles in dramatic and sociodramatic play. It is through movement from the body energies, to the use of toys (and materials), and toys into play that the child learns to become a socially effective worker with others (Freud, 1971).

REFERENCES

Anker, D., Jones, D., & Willison, C. R. (1974). Teaching children as they play. *Young Children, 29,* 203–212.

Brearley, M. (1969). *The teaching of young children: Some applications of Piaget's learning theory.* New York: Schocken Books.

Brissett, D., & Edgley, C. (1975). *Life as theater: A dramaturgical sourcebook.* Chicago: Aldine Publishing.

Curry, N. E. (1974a). Dramatic play as a curriculum tool. In D. Sponseller (Ed.), *Play as a learning medium* (pp. 78–93). Washington, DC: National Association for the Education of Young Children.

Curry, N. E. (1974b). Play in personality development. In M. Almy (Ed.), *Early childhood play: Selected readings related to cognition and motivation*, (pp. 63–78). New York: Simon and Schuster.

Elkisch, P. (1957). Psychological significance of the mirror. *Journal of American Psychoanalytical Association, 5*, 235–244.

Erikson, E. (1950). *Childhood and society.* New York: W. W. Norton.

Freud, A. (1971). *The ego and the mechanisms of defense.* New York: International Universities Press.

Gerhardt, L. A. (1973). *Moving and knowing: The young child orients himself in space.* Upper Saddle River, NJ: Prentice Hall.

Hirsch, E. S. (1974). *The block book.* Washington, DC: National Association for the Education of Young Children.

Montessori, M. (1965). *Dr. Montessori's own handbook.* New York: Schocken Books.

Parten, M. B. (1971). Social play among preschool children. In R. E. Herron and B. Sutton-Smith (Eds.), *Child's play* (pp. 83–95). New York: John Wiley and Sons.

Piaget, J. (1965). *The moral judgement of the child* (trans. Marjorie Gabain). New York: Free Press.

SUGGESTED READINGS

Kritchevsky, S., Prescott, E., & Walling, L. (1969) *Planning environments for young children: Physical space.* Washington, DC: National Association for the Education for Young Children.

Krown, S. (1974). *Threes and fours go to school.* Upper Saddle River, NJ: Prentice Hall.

Lowenfeld, V. (1952). *Creative and mental growth* (3rd ed.). New York: Macmillan.

Matterson, E. M. (1965). *Play with a purpose for under seven.* Baltimore, MD: Penguin Books.

Matterson, E. M. (1973). *Play and playthings for the preschool child.* Baltimore, MD: Penguin Books.

Sears, S. (1972). *The relationship between sociodramatic play and school achievement of second grade low socioeconimic status black children.* Doctoral dissertation, Ohio State University, Columbus, OH.

Smilansky, S. (1968). *The effects of sociodramatic play on disadvantaged preschool children.* New York: John Wiley and Sons.

7 Misbehavior at Snack Time, Circle Time, and Other Daily Time Periods

Why is it that a young child may present no difficulties on the playground where active physical play is encouraged, but the very same child will be disruptive at "circle time," with its demands for sitting quietly and listening to adults and classmates? Other children are well behaved nearly all day, except when they come to the table for snack or mealtime. Then they are transformed from Dr. Jekyll into Mr. Hyde. How should these "misbehaviors" be handled during critical daily time periods?

Nearly every early childhood classroom divides its day: arrival rituals, free-play period, circle or group times, toileting, snack periods, rest or nap periods, and outdoor and indoor times. Within each of these clearly defined time periods and during the transitions in between, acting-out behavior increases, changes in form, or decreases, depending on the demands of that activity. To assist the teacher in dealing with difficult behavior and highly demanding children, presented here are each of the common time periods used in most classroom days, describing the typical misbehavior seen and suggesting concrete actions a teacher may take in handling this misbehavior.

Arrivals

To adults, the movement from home to school or from parent to teacher and classroom seems a simple matter. But for young children, especially for three-year-olds (Freud, 1968; Mahler, Pine, & Bergman, 1975), these changes may have the impact of culture shock (Toffler, 1971). If an adult were transported suddenly to a foreign country with a different language, different foods and ways to eat it, different clothing, and the like, she would be under great stress—culture shock. The school—which is a new place to live and work with others—places similar stress on the young child, who must be wondering to himself: "Where do I go to the potty if I need to? Who will keep me safe here when my mother is gone? Will others take my toys from me? Where do I sleep and eat?"

Stages of Separation Adjustment

This fear of the school as an unknown will produce a variety of behaviors on the child's part. Here is an example of a successful preschool adaptation, with the child progressing through various stages of adjustment (Speers, 1970a, 1970b).

Lap Stage.   Three-year-old Kate enters the classroom door, tightly holding her mother's hand. After child and parent are warmly greeted by the teacher and silently observed by the other children, the full meaning of "going to school" and "mother leaving" begins to come to Kate. She climbs on her mother's lap and buries her face in her mother's chest. For a few minutes she refuses to look at this new world. This is the lap stage of adjustment. The teacher encourages the mother to take the rocking chair to a large upright mirror mounted on the wall and sit with her back to the mirror. When Kate feels more relaxed, the teacher adds, the mother might demonstrate some of the toys to her. Then the teacher leaves, explaining reassuringly that she will be back shortly to help.

Customs Inspection Stage.   Kate stops her crying and begins peeking over her mother's shoulder to watch the classroom activities through the mirror. Kate begins to point things out to her mother, and the two chat about what is occurring. This is the customs inspection stage.

Practicing Stage. After looking around the room for awhile, Kate suddenly slips from her mother's lap, runs out into the classroom to grab a toy, and brings it quickly back to her mother. Then, standing at her mother's knee, she watches to see if anyone will intervene. She makes eye contact with the teacher, who smiles an okay at her.

Kate's mother names the object that Kate retrieved and demonstrates its function. Three or four times Kate runs out, grabs an object, darts back, and puts it in her mother's hands; each time her mother responds by telling her the name of the object and demonstrating its uses. This is the practicing stage—practicing being separated from mother for short periods.

Teacher Approach Stage.   The teacher did not throw herself at the child, but permitted the child and parent time to relax and gradually separate physically. During the gradual separation, the teacher observed the parent-child interaction, noting the sensory modalities employed by the mother.

Is the mother trying to reassure the child by using language to explain, "This is what we are doing," or "this is what will happen next"? If so, this may be a verbal mother.

Is the mother cuddling and caressing the child, as well as exploring objects with her own hands and encouraging the child to do likewise? This may be a tactile mother. Is the mother signaling the child with her eyes, telling her to "go ahead and pick up the object" simply by using her eyes and facial expressions? She may be a visual mother.

The teacher has just learned something about the sensory modality or combination of modalities that she may now use to make this child begin to feel comfortable in her new preschool world. For the hearing-verbal child, the teacher tells what is happening or is going to happen ("We are going to read a book about . . . ," or, "You will sit near me so that you may hear the story"). For the tactile-physical child, the teacher brings a furry puppet or takes the child to the classroom's pet rabbit, encouraging her to touch. For the visual child, the teacher signals with her eyes that there is a free chair, toy, or materials available, and encourages the child to use them. If the child and mother communicate well verbally, but engage in little or no touching, an attempt on the teacher's part to cuddle with or physically cue that child may be seen by the child as frightening or intrusive.

Why is it that when there are two or three teachers in a classroom, each child seems to gain a solid emotional relationship with one or two teachers and will shy away from or reject a relationship with another teacher? It may be that the child and a certain teacher share a form of sensory communication, while the rejected teacher may unknowingly be attempting to communicate in the child's weak or underdeveloped modality. Teachers should attempt to determine their own strong and weak modalities and begin to practice ways of shifting gears deliberately, moving into different modalities to try to communicate with different children. Later in the child's school years, his favored modality may become his best learning style.

Parent Departure Stage.   Once communication is established between child and teacher, the parent may depart with minimal stress for the new child. The preceding example demonstrated initial fearfulness on Kate's part and a demand for her mother to remain. These stress indicators are viewed as positive, because they mean that there is a healthy attachment between child and parent. The crying and demanding are simply an indication of love. If the child is given the time to regress to more infantile behaviors, such as becoming a lap baby, she should gradually emerge from the arms of her mother and be able to join the other children.

Surprisingly, the children who act like "little men" or "little women" and show no emotional stress when the mother departs often have greater difficulty in making good long-term adjustments in the classroom. These children often refuse later to be cuddled or comforted by the teacher, need excessive teacher attention, behave in "run-and-chase" fashion that puts themselves in dangerous situations, and engage in stereotypical play—failing to progress developmentally.

The point is that signs of stress, such as crying and demanding, are normal. The teacher's role is to find ways to bridge the child gradually from home to school. One way this can be done is by giving the parent time to stay with the child in the first hours or days of school. Another way is to provide the child with an ever-present, comforting reminder of the parent—for example, by pinning his mother's handkerchief with her perfume on it to the front of the child's clothing, so the child may touch it and smell "mother" all day long. Or the teacher might permit the child to call his mother by telephone during the day; hearing his mother's voice provides reassurance that she will return. The parent could bring a family photo for the child to keep and show around; or the teacher could let the child bring a transitional object (Winnicott, 1971)—a blanket such as the one cherished by the "Peanuts" character Linus, or a cuddle toy—to carry for the first few days. These transition objects give sensory reminders of home, permanence, and mother, helping the child to make the adjustments from home to school.

Another help in this transition is having the teacher and child play "mommy and child" with the use of a toy telephone. Remember the earlier example of the value of make-believe play for helping children digest difficult emotional experiences—the child making her own fantasy ice cream cones in the sandbox? (See Chapter 1.) With the toy telephone, the teacher carries on a conversation with the child, reassuring him that his mother is thinking about him and will not forget to pick him up at the end of day.

Similar dramas may be played out with puppets, making one puppet the child and the other the parent. In the puppet modeling by the teacher, the child puppet pleads, "Please don't go, Mommy." The mother puppet explains that she must leave to do such and such, and that the teacher will keep him safe until she returns. A teacher puppet now appears and helps the child puppet to go potty, eat, sleep, and play. Finally, a knock is heard at the door and mother puppet has returned to reunite warmly with the child puppet.

Here are some further suggestions for helping children make initial adjustments to school:

1. Have the teacher visit the child's home, watch for parent-child cueing modalities, and learn to communicate with the child on familiar ground.

2. Have the parent and child make a visit to the classroom when no other children are there, possibly after school or on weekends. Have the mother encourage the child to use the small toilets, be seated with teacher and mother for a quick snack, and take toys from the shelf and play with them. Have the child take some object home with him that he will bring back the first day, such as an inexpensive toy, a piece of modeling dough, or a crayon with paper. Label the child's storage cubby or cot with his name and, if possible, a photo. (Note: Some children, when visiting a store where countless enticements sit on display shelves, have been told not to touch and have even been disciplined harshly for not complying. These same children will be afraid to touch or take things stored on shelves in the classroom. Parents and teachers must communicate that it is safe and permitted for them to take and use the classroom objects.)

3. With a small group of already adjusted children, play a series of imitative games, such as Thumbkin or Simon Says. The object of the play activity is for the new child to be directly introduced to a group of children, so they will at least know one another's names.

4. Cut a large silhouette of the new child, paste a photograph of him on it, and display it in a prominent place so all can see it, including parents arriving in the classroom.

5. Prepare the parents for the routine they should follow when they bring in the child for the first time. Explain to them that the school views the early signs of stress as positive, and that they should expect the stages of separation, lap,

customs inspection, and practicing before the teacher approach stage. Remind the parent, though, that some children might not go through these separation processes the first day of school, but may wait until later in the school year, after a long weekend or holiday period.

Some parents say, "He did so well the first two weeks, but now he doesn't want to come to school and makes a fuss!" The child is just now beginning to truly separate; if the parents are aware of this beforehand, they will not be disturbed by these new behaviors. Parents may consider removing the child from the school, if they have not been previously warned to expect some stress.

Snack and Eating Times

Mid-morning and mid-afternoon snacks not only provide nourishment for highly active young children but also bring them together to further a sense of group belonging. Businesspeople take clients to lunch, families gather for holiday dinners—sharing food in pleasant settings creates a sense of belonging. It is critical that snack time be a pleasant experience for children because, if it is not, the situation may give rise to competition and aggression. Eating periods are not times for teachers to have breaks, leaving behind the less trained and less experienced teachers or aids to carry on. If negative instances occur at home between parent and child, they will most likely occur at the dinner table or at the child's bedtime. Therefore, preschool eating at snack time and lunchtime (as well as nap time) are prime periods for the children to become difficult, expecting to carry out power struggles with teachers just as they do with parents at home.

In organizing for snack time, the concepts of control of error and degrees of freedom are used. Children should not be allowed to play with food; they should be encouraged to become accustomed to a routine that is nonrepressive and is easy to follow.

Here is an example of what *not* to do at snack time: The teacher instructs a mature child to set out the napkins and cups before each chair at the table. The children come to their seats, which are marked with their names. The teacher, seated at the end of the table, makes an announcement or, where appropriate, says grace. Then, extending a wicker basket of food such as celery or cookies—but not permitting the children to pass the basket—the teacher instructs each child to take one. (If any food remains in the basket, it is removed from the table so the children will not fight over it.) The children are instructed to set the snack on their napkin and wait until all are ready to eat. Next, the teacher appears with a pitcher of milk or juice and, moving behind the children, fills their paper cups. After the teacher is again seated, the children are told they may begin. They are required to eat and drink everything they have been given and to wait at the table until everyone else is finished. One child then travels around the table gathering the used cups and napkins.

This is the classroom kingdom, where the teacher rules. Such a rigid snacking procedure indicates that the teacher does not believe children can learn responsibility and has an overriding fear that an accident will occur. The teacher shows a limited understanding of control of error as she plays food server to passive children.

Snack materials should be engineered to allow children to eat with minimal pressures from adults. First, two plastic containers with pouring lids, each holding approximately three cups of juice or milk, are placed on a cafeteria tray, along with two snack-filled wicker baskets lined with napkins and a stack of three-ounce drinking cups. The lidded pouring containers will help keep spills to a minimum. Also on the tray are napkins in a weighted holder (this will keep the napkins from blowing away when snack time takes place outdoors). Approximately 30 percent more snacks than there are children should be provided. These items are previously prepared by the teacher (or the cook, if the school is fortunate enough to have one).

The responsibility—and opportunity—for bringing the filled cafeteria tray to the table belongs to the children who have finished cleanup from previous activities and have washed their hands. They bring the tray carefully from the kitchen to the center of the snack table. Round tables, each seating eight children, are ideal in that they enable each child to see the faces of all the others and have equal access to the cafeteria tray. Rectangular tables tend to leave the end child out of conversations and access. After washing up, the children seat themselves as desired, select napkins and cups from the center of the table, pour their own juice or milk, and pass the container to a neighbor. Snack items are then taken from the basket with plastic prongs (for health reasons) and passed from one child to another. Children are permitted to take more than one food item, and the three-ounce cups make it necessary for them to refill their cups repeatedly. The teacher sits at the table or at a nearby table and models behavior by carrying on light conversations, and eating and drinking the snack just as she wishes the children to do. Coffee cups and soda cans used by the teacher at the snack table would be inappropriate modeling. When children have had enough food and conversation, they may get up at will, drop their napkins and cups in plastic-lined waste cans nearby, and move to some quiet activity, such as reading or looking at picture books. This procedure gives the children freedom and control. The teacher is not a food server or boss, but an equal member of the group.

Open Snack

At some child-centered programs the children are all herded together for snack, regardless of whether they are ready to eat. Why not give the children total autonomy over eating by arranging an open snack? From 9:00 A.M. until 10:30 A.M., a child-sized table with two chairs is placed in the corner of the classroom, arranged with snack materials as described, with three-ounce cups, lidded pouring containers, and snacks in baskets—but this time the basket is covered with a see-through plastic lid with a handle. A child is free during this open snack period to find a friend, wash hands (a container with soapy water and a supply of paper towels are nearby), and eat a snack when desired. The only rule is that the child must bring a friend. If he can't find a friend that morning, the teacher may eat with the child—and then engineer socially to help that child make a friend in the next few weeks.

On the wall near the open snack table is a class roster where the teacher keeps a record of the time each child eats snack, and with whom. Open snack is especially useful during the beginning of a school year, when many children are making an initial adjustment; it may be alternated with group snack for variety so that the children may benefit from the advantages of both methods.

Eating Difficulties

Some children begin to act out when they come to a group sitting to eat. These carry-over behaviors from home are rooted in power struggles and generally are seen in the form of the child who will not eat or the child who becomes aggressive verbally (calling others names) and physically (jabbing others with a finger), harasses others, and hoards snacks.

This "misbehavior" should be seen as a sign of basic insecurity and fear of the eating and group situation. Such acting-out children should not be viewed simply as bullies or as just being mean. The goal is to have each child become comfortable enough to eat and socialize with others.

The teacher may start by permitting the difficult child to eat in a one-to-one relationship with a friend or adult at a small table. This should not be done in such a manner that the child views it as isolation or punishment, but as a special time with a friend or teacher. Later, a second child can be invited to the small table, with others gradually joining over a period of days or weeks until the child finally is eating with a group. Even after the child has adjusted to the large group setting, there may be bad days when he might be permitted to revert to a smaller group for eating.

While he is making these initial adjustments, few eating demands should be made of the child; the teacher should depend on the other children to be good models of behavior for the difficult child. If he refuses to eat, the teacher makes no demands, simply cleaning up when snack is over and moving on to other activities. Some teachers worry that if the child has not eaten he will become malnourished; however, the failure to eat at school will only occur over a two- to three-week period, and with a well-balanced day of active play the child will develop a healthy appetite. When the child who won't eat knows that the pressure is off, he will eat. Teachers must have faith that this will occur.

It is not surprising to discover that it is the difficult child's parents who are most likely to demand at the end of the day a full report of the child's eating performance. This is symptomatic of a power struggle between parent and child at mealtime. The parents' emotional intensity may be strong and possibly intimidating to the teacher, attempting to draw her into the power struggle. But the teacher's response to the parent should be a statement of encouragement: "He did better today!" or, "He is becoming more comfortable at snack and gradually eating more; we are confident that in a few days he will be eating a full serving." The teacher then moves on to other positive topics with the parent, telling of the other activities in which the child is doing well. Modeling positive expectations for the child is the best support the teacher can give to parents who appear to be overly concerned.

Dealing With the Aggressive Child

For the hoarding child who takes far too much from the shared snack basket, in the initial period the teacher provides items that are very small, such as nuts, dry cereals, or trail mix, rather than large items, such as muffins. The teacher states, "Take all that you can eat and leave in the basket all that you cannot eat. You may take seconds, and I will always make sure that everyone gets enough to eat." Remember from the chapter on discipline and child guidance (Chapter 3), the rule is to tell the child what to do, not what *not* to do. The teacher must resist the natural tendency to state, "Don't take so much, Tommy. You are not going to eat all of that." She permits the child, for a period of days or even two to three weeks, to continue to hoard without any comment. The hoarder has a basic "not okay" view of the world, and his life-stance is that the world is denying him and he must fight to get his needs met.

At the end of snack, during cleanup, the teacher appears before the hoarding child (who will have a large pile of snacks in front of him uneaten), make eye contact, touch the remaining food with her hand to focus his attention on what she is talking about, and then reassuringly repeats, "Take all that you can eat and leave in the basket all that you cannot eat. You may take seconds, and I will always make sure that everyone gets enough to eat." Over the next weeks the teacher begins to progress back down the Teacher Behavioral Continuum (TBC) with the hoarding child:

Acting.   The teacher eats with others who exhibit good eating behaviors.

Commanding.   Before the child takes from the basket of food, the teacher states directly, "Take all that you can eat and leave in the basket all that you cannot eat. You may take seconds, and I will always make sure that everyone gets enough to eat."

Questioning.   Again, just before the child takes from the shared basket, the teacher poses the question, "Tommy, what is our rule about taking snacks from the basket?"

Naming.   The teacher states to the group in general, as the basket is passed, "We have a rule for taking snacks." Such nondirective or naming reminders simply bring the desired rule to the child's awareness before he acts.

Looking.   Difficult children need the teacher nearby during snack, radiating a zone of safety and control. If a teacher must supervise a number of tables, she may choose to eat at the table where the target child is seated for a number of weeks. This looking on is not done with an attitude of, "I have to keep an eye on him every moment or he will get out of hand," but rather the attitude must be that the teacher wants a close, positive relationship with the child.

Acting Out While Eating

Once the child has become relaxed and adjusted to eating with others, there will be times when he or other members of the class may begin to disrupt the eating situa-

FIGURE 7.1   Snacking/Eating (Teacher Behavioral Continuum)

Looking	Naming	Questioning	Commanding	Acting (physical intervention)
Radiating a zone of safety and control	"We have a rule for taking snacks."	"Jim, what is our rule about taking snacks from baskets?"	"Take all that you can eat and leave in the basket all that you cannot eat. You may take seconds, and I will always make sure that everyone gets enough to eat."	Teacher and peers model appropriate eating behavior

tion in a manner that necessitates direct action by the teacher. This will be done by escalating back up the TBC (see Figure 7.1).

Carol has been silly all morning, giggling, challenging the limits imposed by the teacher, and generally refusing to fit into routines. At snack time, she is excessively loud, prevents the child next to her from eating by calling her names, and makes the entire eating atmosphere unpleasant.

The teacher changes her seat location, moving into the direct view of Carol (looking). If need be, she touches Carol or uses other nonverbal actions to make the child aware that she is present. A simple looking might get Carol back on track; if not, the teacher escalates up the continuum.

The teacher announces in a nondirective naming statement, "At snack time we need to remember to use our 'inside' voices." (naming)

The teacher increases the intervention by moving up the continuum to questioning: "Do you need my help to remember rules at snack?" or, "Do you need to move to a smaller, quieter table to be able to eat your snack this morning, Carol?"

If Carol continues to be defiant, the teacher follows with a preparatory command or promise to take action in the form of a consequence. "Carol (uses name, touches her on shoulder, and makes direct eye contact), I want you to turn around, sit up in your chair, put your food in your mouth, and use an 'inside' voice that does not hurt ears." She remains defiant. "If I see that done again, it is telling me that you do not know the rules for eating snacks with others, and I will ask you to move to another table, or leave snack time this morning." (logical consequence)

If the child continues to refuse, the teacher now intervenes physically (acting), if need be, to move the child away from the situation in a nonpunitive manner. (See Chapter 4 on discipline and child guidance for techniques in handling temper tantrums, which are likely to occur when very strong intervention is used.)

Rest or Nap Time

It is recommended that for all-day programs, three- and four-year-old children might require at least two hours or more of afternoon rest or sleep, while five-year-olds might need a minimum of forty-five minutes in quiet, lie-down-on-a-mat rest. Resting is another area in which power struggles often occur between parents or other adults and the child, and these patterns will often be brought into the school during sleeping and resting periods.

Again, children (and adults) live in three worlds: an inside world of thought and feelings, where the focus of attention is internal; a body world, which includes physical activities such as swimming, running, or simply relaxing in a bathtub; and an external world, which includes all things outside the individual. A healthy form of regression for an adult at the end of a very busy day is to crawl into a large, comfortable chair, kick off tight shoes, and relax (the body world); then, take time to daydream or think over the day (the inside world). Adults and children move in and out of these three worlds throughout the day.

In order to sleep, young children must give up being attuned to the external world of others and objects, move through the body world by feeling themselves physically relax, and then move into an inner world of thoughts that finally lead to unconscious sleep. Overactive children, children frightened by a new school situation, or children who have patterns of engaging in power conflicts centered on napping will not be able to move back normally through these three worlds. Thus, the rest period is not a time to be left to inexperienced staff; teachers need to be present—to rub backs, to talk to children, to reassure them with their presence that the children are safe and secure.

The difficult child, when asked to lie on a cot, cannot give up an external awareness because his perceptions are outward and defensive. To help counter this, each child should have a cot labeled with his name, located at the same spot each day (for health reasons, children should not sleep on each other's cots). This is truly a private space, and other children should not be permitted to invade it by putting their hands or feet on the cots. The teachers should distribute themselves around the sleep area, kneeling near the children who are having difficulty relaxing and helping them with appropriate sensory measures. Soft music without lyrics can be played to mask inside and outside noise. Some children may be permitted to wear headphones to listen to soft music to screen out external sounds; but teachers must be careful, especially if wires are connected to the headphones, to remove them once the child is asleep.

The child who is visually stimulated may be placed near a wall, shelving, or small movable screen, so that distractions will be kept from view. For some tactile children, gentle back rubbing will help bring on relaxation. Once the children are relaxed and quieted, teachers may depart the sleeping room, leaving behind one adult, who will always be seated in the same location during rest. This is important, because children will awaken, look to the "adult chair," see the teacher, be reassured, and return to sleep. If that chair is deserted, the child sits up to look for the teacher and will have a very difficult time getting to sleep again.

There are rare children at this age who seem not to need sleep. Their behavior and personality are productive throughout the school day; for them being on a cot is like being in jail. An attempt shoud be made to get such a child to rest and sleep, but if he cannot after fifteen to twenty minutes and after attempts to help him relax, he can be given a picture book or miniature toy to use quietly on his cot. Then, if the child still acts as if he is in jail, the teacher may permit him to leave the sleeping room quietly and do some tabletop activities (clay modeling or drawing, for example) in another room. A reprimand will only cause the child greater tension and make it even more difficult for him to relax. This would be a real contradiction of the teacher's goal.

Circle or Story Time

Bringing together a group of five-, four-, and especially three-year-old children and getting them to focus their full attention on one adult takes great care and technical understanding. Group time provides third-sphere communication (one to all), in which the teacher requires all attention to focus on her while her emotions and responses are diffused to all members of a group—generally not to one child. Thus, each child is required to inhibit his own egocentric desires and become a part of the collective activity. This is socially very demanding for the young child, who is still quite self-centered. The teacher must carefully regulate the amount of time children will be required to maintain themselves in nonpersonal, directly controlled situations. Circle or story time is one such situation. If well managed, this activity can lead the child toward a greater ability to handle direct instruction.

The transition into and out of group time is critical. If all children in a preschool class run into the circle or story room, trying to grab a favorite spot, pushing and shoving will occur with some danger of minor injury.

The following example points to a better way of making a transition from, for example, snack time to circle time (see Figure 7.2). The teacher in charge of circle time collects three to six children who have finished with their previous activity and

FIGURE 7.2   **Making Good Transitions**

- Generally, never have young children stand in line to wait.
- Move children in groups of three to six, with the first group accompanied by the "point" teacher, who has these children get the new area ready for those to follow.
- The last teacher to leave the space, such as the room where story time is held, asks the remaining three to six children to clean up before moving them to the new location.
- When children are making transitions to a new space, before they leave their present space they should know where they are going and what they will do when they get there.

have cleaned up. She directs them to follow her to the rug in the circle room or area. Once at the rug the teacher must take a power position, much like a judge in a courtroom, placing herself higher than the children, on a piano stool, rocking chair, or similar seat.

Circle time must be engineered with an understanding of control of error. Each child should know the rules about what he should and shouldn't do, and there must be some definition of individual seating space. Two large half-circles, taped or painted, or a circle design in the rug indicate where each child is to be seated with legs tucked under. The first children will take the inner circle, closest to the teacher, while the later children will take the back circle, refraining from stepping on children already seated. The motor rules and circle on the floor are structured to control error; if there is no structure, the children will be randomly scattered over the rug, rolling over, lying down, and getting up and down—all in all, a recipe for potential chaos.

The teacher should not wait until everyone is present and ready (this would cause the waiting children to find negative ways of amusing themselves), but should simply start off with a finger game, songs with physical actions, or something similar. Once everyone has come in, a storybook can be begun.

While circle time is in progress, other teachers or aids need to be present at the back of the circle. If certain children cannot relax and begin to disrupt the story, the helping teachers would move closer to them and touch them on their backs or draw them into their own laps, generally helping them to relax. Or these teachers may, in the case of very physically active children, move them to child-sized chairs at the edge of the circle. These children literally hold themselves onto the chairs until they gain control of their bodies.

If repetitive disruptions by one or more children do occur, the teacher who is reading or carrying on the activity must take some action, and that action will be based on the TBC.

The teacher may simply signal with her eyes (looking) to the off-task child that she wants his or her attention. This is also a signal to the helping teacher on the sidelines to move in and help with this child. At this point it is important for the teacher to understand the concept of high-profile and low-profile correction in a directive teaching situation. Stopping the activities to reprimand one child directly disrupts the shared fantasy of the story for all others, as well as possibly making the other children feel empathetically tense and uncomfortable. "John, you are not listening and you are disrupting the story for everyone." The eyes of all other children now turn to John. This high-profile correction is a guilt-inducing statement. The reprimand has probably disrupted the story more than John's original actions did. In using low-profile correction the teacher simply looks at John, says his name, and points out some aspect of the book or object she is sharing. "John, you will notice (pointing to the picture) that the troll is hiding under the bridge." Using low-profile corrections, the teacher uses the child's name, her hand, and visual focus but continues with the rhythms of the story.

If disruption by the difficult child continues, the teacher moves up the TBC to questioning and to even more directive actions that require a high profile. But when two or more adults are teaching in the classroom, the in-charge teacher can depend on the sideline teacher to help with children who need a visual signal (looking). The teacher then questions all children, "What are our rules of behavior at circle time?" She then commands, "Show me that you know the rules!" Finally comes a preparatory command to the off-task child: "John, you are showing me this morning that you have not learned the rules for story time, and if . . . occurs again, I will ask you to go to the next room and choose something else to do."

If the misbehavior continues, the in-charge teacher directs the sideline teacher to remove John from circle time (acting). Because a very high-profile correction is needed, the teacher may choose to stop the story and play a finger or hand game, and then reintroduce the story. Later, in a nonpunitive manner, the in-charge teacher approaches John, moving through the TBC again, with child and teacher seated in chairs facing each other knee to knee (looking). "You have had a really difficult time in circle time this morning." (naming). "What are the rules for circle time?" (questioning) "In circle time I want you to sit on your spot on the line, look at me, and listen to the story." (commanding) If the teacher feels that the child truly does not understand the rules, the two of them could go to the rug room and the teacher could reteach the rules (acting). This knee-to-knee follow-through lets the child know, in a nonpunitive manner, exactly what is wanted.

Departing from circle time can be done quickly and in an orderly manner. Children generally should be dismissed in groups of six to eight. The in-charge teacher may continue with a simple hand game, while the sideline teacher signals a small group of children and leads them to a definite location. The in-charge teacher dismisses another group of six to eight, directing them to go to the sideline teacher at her location. Finally, the in-charge teacher has the remaining children clean up the room and then follow her to the new location. Notice that no child has had to stand in line. Waiting in lines should be a real "no-no" in early childhood practice. Children at this age do not move well in herds!

Other Key Considerations

Even as the day is divided into specific time periods for different activities, certain features recur throughout the school day and must be planned for.

Active/Passive Times.   Consider the amount of physical activity of the child and try to balance this with a passive activity. Children tend to get stuck in outside or physical worlds and cannot slow down and relax. Some young children, if permitted, would continue to be drunk with running and movement until they were so exhausted they would actually drop in their tracks. Once children have had enough activity, they should be moved to story time, puzzles, or similar sedentary activities.

Outside Climate and Weather.   To balance outside and inside activities, the teacher must be aware of the general climate and be prepared to make daily adjustments. In tropical climates during the summer months, the teacher may wish to have the outside time in the early mornings when it is relatively cool and stay indoors in the afternoon. The opposite is true for cold climates or winter months, when the teacher may decide to stay inside in the mornings and go outside in the afternoon in the warmer sun.

Preparing for Outdoor Activities.   Helping children put on their coats one at a time as the others wait is a fertile time for conflict to occur between children. You may teach young children to put on their own coats or jackets independently and quickly by taking the following steps:

1. Have them place their coat on a table with the button (or zipper) up and the coat on its back, with the collar facing the child.
2. Have the child place his hands into the sleeves (right hand to right sleeve, left hand into left sleeve) while the coat is still on the table, and then raise the coat and hands over his head, keeping his arms straight.
3. Have him slide his arms down into the sleeves as he drops his arms.

Departure

There are some children who do well all day long, until the first parent appears at the end of the day to pick up her child. Then the Dr. Jekyll and Mr. Hyde syndrome appears among some of the remaining children, with crying, temper tantrums, and defiance toward the teacher. Why is this so? After the first parent of the day comes for her child, the "Mr. Hyde" child may worry about whether he will be picked up by his own parents. For him the question is, "Will my mom forget me?" This is not an extraordinary worry, but it will be a concern for all children at this age.

The goal is to occupy the children's minds (perhaps with a story) and possibly their hands (using structured construction materials, such as puzzles) in some activity that keeps their minds off their worry and separation fears. This can be done by having a small, intimate circle time with the six to eight children who are picked up late. Find a comfortable corner on a rug where children can sit on the teacher's lap or otherwise be physically close to the teacher. Read stories, play hand games, and carry on lively conversation, permitting individual children to depart from the circle at natural break points when the teacher is aware that the parent has arrived. This should be done whenever the parent is truly late. Simply leaving the last child on his own to attend to cleanup chores will give that child a real feeling of loss. The teacher should engage him, if possible, in helping clean up or take time for some one-to-one communication until the parent arrives.

Summary

Techniques have been presented for smoother handling of arrivals, snack eating, meal patterns, rest time, circle or story time, transitions, departures, schedules, and teaching motor rules. These techniques are founded on the underlying premise that children can be trusted and that their inappropriate actions stem from their lack of ability to behave as we desire. The objective is to give them a secure environment where they can learn these skills and move forward in their development.

To accomplish this task, the teacher needs to understand how to arrange a well-balanced classroom, allowing for freedom and control of error. Once a well-designed play environment is created, and the child understands the motor rules and time schedules, the classroom runs smoothly without the need for excessive teacher control. The teacher is then free to facilitate the children's ongoing play, usually through the TBC, to further their journey toward effectiveness, autonomy, and increased maturity.

REFERENCES

Freud, A. (1968). *Normality and pathology in childhood: Assessments of development.* New York: International Universities Press.

Mahler, M.S., Pine, S., & Bergman, A. (1975). *The psychological birth of the human infant.* New York: Basic Books.

Speers, R. W., Curry, N., & Armand, S. (1970a). Recapitulation of separation-individuation process when the normal three-year-old enters nursery school. In J. McDevitt (Ed.), *Separation-individuation: Essays in honor of Margaret Mahler* (pp. 57–86). New York: International Universities Press.

Speers, R.W., et al. (1970b). *Variations in separation-individuation and implications for play ability and learning as studied in the three-year-old in nursery school.* Pittsburgh: University of Pittsburgh Press.

Toffler, A. (1971). *Future shock.* New York: Bantam Books.

Winnicott, D. W. (1971). *Playing and reality.* London: Travistock Publications.

SUGGESTED READINGS

Dreikurs, R. (1964). *Children: The challenge.* New York: Hawthorn Books.

Freud, A. (1971). *The ego and the mechanisms of defense.* New York: International Universities Press.

Mahler, M. S. (1970). *On human symbiosis and the vicissitudes of individuation.* New York: International Universities Press.

Wolfgang, C. & Wolfgang, M. E. (1992). *School for young children: Developmentally appropriate practices.* Boston: Allyn and Bacon.

8 Helping Parents Guide Their Difficult Child

The early childhood classroom is often the first institution that can give parents their first normative evaluation of their own child. Parents of aggressive/passive or verbally aggressive children often begin to feel that their child's behaviors are outside their own abilities to handle, and they often seek a quality early childhood center to help them address the behaviors of the difficult child. The noncompliance of the passive child or the raw aggression that parents see often confuses and frustrates them. They have not had the opportunity to see their child among many other children of their own age and have very little or no feel for normal behaviors. They often, understandably, worry as to the normality of their child's behaviors and seek help from child experts.

The parent who sees these nonproductive behaviors at home on a daily basis begins to feel helpless in dealing with the passive child, defeated by the hurtful behaviors of the aggressive child, or annoyed by the child's excessive demands (Dreikurs, 1964). The young child and his behaviors are most challenging to young and possibly inexperienced parents, who may require specialized parent training to help them learn to deal effectively with their feelings toward their own child and to gain new skills for coping with these difficult and challenging children. Early childhood teachers are in a position to recommend strategies and to direct parents to appropriate training so they may gain practical parenting skills.

Today's parents seeking help to understand and to deal with their difficult children are surrounded by the many so-called child experts who inundate them with a host of child guidance books featured on television talk shows and appearing on the shelves of major book stores. Parent training books and training systems can be overwhelming. How can teachers counsel parents as to what philosophy, models, or psychological theories might be most helpful?

Parents' Beliefs About Discipline (Guidance) Inventory

To give orderliness to these child guidance books, theories, and models is a simple survey, the Parent's Beliefs about Discipline (Guidance) Inventory (see Figure 8.1). The inventory asks parents to choose between two competing statements and then,

FIGURE 8.1   Parents' Beliefs About Discipline (Guidance) Inventory

This inventory is designed for parents to assess their own beliefs on discipline and child guidance. It enables the parent to determine the child guidance model or system that they most wish to use. In each numbered question, you are asked to choose between two competing value statements. With some questions, you will definitely like one statement and dislike the second, and it will be easy to decide. With others, you will like or dislike both, leaving you with a frustrating choice—but you must still choose.

Step 1

Instruction: Select A or B to indicate the item you value most. You must choose between the two statements for each. Circle item A or B.

1.	a.	Because young children's thinking is limited, rules need to be established for them by parents.
	b.	I always respect my young children's emotional desires and nearly always go with their choices.
2.	a.	My child might lose privileges for breaking rules.
	b.	My child and I negotiate rules until I get a commitment from him that these rules will be followed.
3.	a.	I give my young child opportunities to make his own choices. When these choices do not work out, I ask him to evaluate his past actions and to consider new choices if this same problem should occur in the future.
	b.	Children (including mine) sometimes do not fully understand the possible negative consequences of their choices; therefore I make most choices for my child at this young age.
4.		*When my young child is playing loudly with his or her toys in the next room:*
	a.	I tell the child that this loudness is over the line, but let him decide on an idea for change, and then we come to an agreement.
	b.	I tell him about the loudness, its effect on me, and my feelings about it— generally I am confident he will change his behavior after he understands this.
5.		*My child is having a friend visit and they have a conflict, both physically pulling at a toy that each wants to use:*
	a.	I tell the children that I will put the toy in "time-out" for fifteen minutes, and if they are able to play without conflict for that time period the item will be returned to them.
	b.	I have the children settle it between themselves by my simply standing nearby asking questions on how they might solve this problem themselves.
6.		*If my child feels that I am being unfair to him, but I disagree with him, then:*
	a.	The child and I will talk about it, both contributing to a list of other alternative solutions, and we would both decide on one or more actions acceptable to both of us.
	b.	I would ask, "What did you do? What is the family rule? How will you act differently the next time?" Then I would ask him to reason through the situation as to how he might act differently if a similar situation would arise.

FIGURE 8.1 (*continued*)

7.		*When a child does not want to go on a family outing*
	a.	I would determine what he really wants and then begin a reward system of having him earn "chips" or points to "buy" that object. A host of house chores, other duties, and full participation on this family outing would earn "chips" that could be use to buy the item he treasures.
	b.	I would arrange something to follow after the family outing that he loves (possibly stopping for ice cream, pizza, or other treats) and then with this awareness of the treat he may choose not to go to the outing. He would stay with a neighbor (anyone he prefers), but he will also miss out on the activity (ice cream, pizza, etc.) that will follow the outing.
8.		*When my child begins to have playmates over, I will most likely*
	a.	Announce the "house" rules and inform them how the rules will be fairly enforced.
	b.	Let them play freely, and if difficulties happen that affect me and my property, I would discuss the effects on me, and have discussions with the children to work on a rule that we can all accept.
9.	a.	I encourage my child to express his ideas and feelings freely even if his comments are at times harsh, with critical words including anger directed at me.
	b.	I encourage the child to come up with choices, select one, and commit himself to it, but I make sure that he does not hurt others or take others' rights away.
10.		*If my child interrupts an important conversation, I will most likely:*
	a.	Ignore my child at this first incident, but begin working through consequences (positive or negative) to teach him not to do this in a future situation.
	b.	Express how the behavior (interruption) has caused me a problem and express my strong feeling of frustration regarding such actions—with this knowledge he will most likely change.
11.		*When a child breaks a rule, a good parent*
	a.	Firmly follows up with an appropriate action that will teach him not to do it again.
	b.	Has him think up actions to "make right" the situation that resulted from his behavior.
12.		*If child refuses to eat any item off his plate at dinner, saying he doesn't like what has been prepared, I would*
	a.	Hold a meeting with him, possibly involving the other members of the family, to decide what meats, vegetables, and other foods are liked by most family members, and these agreed-upon foods are cooked most often.
	b.	No "nagging" is done by me, the parent, toward my child during the meal, but when the table is later cleared, his plate, full of food, is set aside, and the child might return to it later in the evening. But that evening no snacks, or other food treats, would be permitted.

(continued)

FIGURE 8.1 (*continued*)

Step 2

After you have completed the inventory, match the circles answered with the number and circle on the Scoring Form. Then add down the column and establish the percentage for each (rules-consequences, relationship-listening, and confronting-contracting) using the percentage chart.

SCORING FORM

Question	Rules-Rewards	Relationship-Listening	Confronting-Contracting
1.	a.	b.	
·2.	a.		b.
3.	b.		a.
4.		b.	a.
5.	a.	b.	
6.		a.	b.
7.	a.		b.
8.	b.	a.	
9.		a.	b.
10.	a.	b.	
11.	a.		b.
12.		a.	b.
Total: (add down the column)			
Score the percentage for that column (use chart below)			

PERCENTAGE CHART

Total:	0	1	2	3	4	5	6	7	8
%	0%	11%	25%	37%	50%	61%	75%	82%	100%

How to Use & Interpret

The column (rules-rewards, relationship-listening, and confronting-contracting) with the largest number of responses or percentage number is the predominant belief or philosophy that you, the parent, might use. You may wish to read books about or get training on these philosophies (see Appendix A for a list of books, and Appendix B for Internet resources).

when results are tabulated, gives them a general understanding of their own philosophy and feel for the need for control. The inventory clusters and divides parents' attitudes related to their beliefs, based on the relationship-listening model (Gordon, 1974), the confronting-contracting model (Dreikurs, 1964), or the rules-consequences (or rules-rewards) model (behavioral analysis).

Parent Personality Fit

Consider the concept of parent personality through the following example of two mothers. Mother 1 and Mother 2 are feeding their eleven-month-old children, who are sitting on a high chair.

> Mother 1 prepares and stores all warm and cold food on a counter nearby, covers herself completely with an apron, has a moist towel nearby, and puts a bib on the infant. Mother 1 feeds the child one spoonful at a time, making sure that all food gets into the child's mouth and is swallowed. Mother 1 is not harsh but uses fun games like "open up the tunnel (child's mouth), here comes the train (a spoonful of peas)" and her warm and gracious personality to get the food into the infant with no spills or mess. The infant enjoys the process. Mother 1 by her action needs to be in control, and by her behavior follows a series of rules or has a structure as to how things should be done. Mother 1 has structured for control of error (no messes or accidents) but gives limited or no degrees of freedom (child autonomy) for the child to deviate from the routine.

> Mother 2 covers the floor under the high chair with a sheet of plastic, dresses the child in a diaper and small shirt, places the food on a serving tray with suction cups, which is suctioned down to the high chair's table, gives the infant a spoon, shows him how to use it. She permits him to feed himself with his hands while carrying on a "conversation" with the child as she works nearby. The infant, using mostly his hands, gets a third of the food his mouth, a third on himself, and the other third on the floor. The child enjoys the eating experience. Mother 2 is not upset by this messiness and has observed to see that the infant has had adequate food. She puts the child's shirt into the wash, kisses her child warmly, places him in a bath, and hoses off the plastic sheet for the next time. Mother 2 grants the infant much autonomy, or self-control, but is not naive or permissive. She has structured for control of error by covering the floor with plastic, dressing the child for the occasion, and organizing the suction feeding bowl so the food would not get knocked from the high chairs, but she also has granted the child a near total degree of freedom for carrying out this feeding activity. Both mothers have communicated with the child in a warm, supportive manner.

What if a teacher tries to help a parent with a difficult child by suggesting to someone like Mother 1, Mrs. Control, a guidance book and philosophy requiring the parent to give maximum freedom to the child to establish rules and sanctions?

Would there be a personality fit with this parent? The answer is no. What if Mother 2, Mrs. Autonomy, were required to use an obedience model? Would there be a fit here? Most likely the answer is again no.

The problem arises when parents are asked to be something that they are not. Parents tend to mother the way they were mothered and most likely guide and discipline children the way they were taught—this is a projection of personality structure. Parents have a personality core, the "child in them," based on the way they were raised, and they draw on this core when they interact socially with others. They have varying degrees of need for control and rules to guide their interaction with others, including their own children. That core personality will most likely be who they are for the rest of their life, but with some minor change as they mature.

Establishing rules as parents in their homes and setting limits with young children are projections of their personality core. Suggesting books or parent training techniques that are diametrically opposed to their personality core will make their actions false, mechanical, and ineffective—it won't work. Some of the child guidance models, because of the degrees of power and the development of rules, are a mismatch to a given parent's own personality core, and there is a lack of personality fit.

There is a continuum of guidance or discipline models, and all of these established models are of value. No one should dictate to parents which model to use; they must find the model that fits their personality. Mrs. Control might be viewed as strict when dealing with her child, while Mrs. Autonomy might be called a softy in her parent-child interactions, but both of these parents appear to be effective and loved by their children. It is a third type, Mrs. Waffle, that has the serious discipline difficulties—especially when dealing with the very difficult young child. One time she strongly disciplines a child for breaking the rules. The next day she says nothing when the same rule is broken. Mrs. Waffle is not fair, firm, or consistent. The child can never tell where she is coming from—she waffles. She is unpredictable and will be ineffective in providing guidance to the difficult child. As a result, the difficult child begins to make Mrs. Waffle feel hurt, defeated, ineffectual, and resentful. She may become harsh and punitive.

When parents set limits, such as saying "no" or physically intervening in a skilled manner, they help the young child to channel his behavior into safe and proper actions. When these limits are set skillfully, the young child begins to understand that the parent is helping him be safe and thus internalizes the "no's" or limits, which will be seen as a fully developed conscience near the age of six or seven (Erikson, 1950; Piaget, 1965).

Limit setting is one of the central variables in helping a young child acquire a healthy self-concept. Consider the following two mothers as they set limits with their toddlers.

Mother 1 and her child are at grandmother's house, which is not a child-proofed space. Jonathan, her toddler son, spies a treasured, breakable knick-nack on a low end table. His eyes widen, and he bolts to get hold of the heirloom. Mother 1 arrives at the table at the same time, having been keeping an eye on him. "Oh, Jonathan, I see that you have found Grandma's Hummel figurine. Let's take a look at it." Mother 1 gently and in a very slow and dramatic manner picks up the figure and moves to the floor in front of Jonathan, who is now seated. He reaches out and fingers the object with great interest as his mother explains what it is, using a wide variety of adjectives to describe the object. After a period of seven to eight minutes, the child begins to lose interest and stands up to leave and find another object that interests him. Mother 1 states, "Look, Jonathan, this is Grandma's very special figurine. Now let's put it back in its safe place. If you want to see it again, come and get me and I will help you look at it safely." Jonathan never shows further interest, nor does he touch the figurine again.

In a similar setting, the child of Mother 2 bolts toward a similar precious object. "No, James, No! Do not touch that—that's Grandma's and it's not a toy." The toddler is still interested and moves to the object. "No! Don't touch that!" Mother 2 repeats. James reaches out, pointing at the object. Mother 2 moves quickly to James and slaps him smartly on the hand, and again states, "You heard me. I said no!" James throws himself on the floor in a full-blown temper tantrum, crying intensely and flailing his arms and legs.

In these and 1,001 similar incidences of limit setting from the age of twelve months through ages four, five and six, the nonskilled mother—Mother 2—communicates to her young child that this *is* or *is not* a safe, interesting world that may be enjoyed, understood, and managed. For James, the world for him as a toddler is like walking into a minefield. Things that he will do but that he cannot yet understand, will trigger a spanking or other harsh action that will cause him physical pain and great stress. Add in the accumulation of the daily accidents that normally befall a developing toddler to gain a picture of the world of frustration for children such as James. Gradually his demeanor and actions appear as if he is suffering battle fatigue. He is learning to mistrust the world and feel guilty for his actions and behavior and to have a growing doubt in his own abilities. If this continues, James is likely to develop a poor self-concept.

In Defense of Parents

James and his mother are presented for purposes of example, not to heave burden and blame on parents. Many children are born difficult if not impossible to mother or parent (Escalona, 1968). Negative interactions between mother and child may not be understandable outside the context of the past history of incidents and circumstances. There are prenatal variables (genetic temperament, prenatal effects of medication, etc.), the birth process (use of forceps causing early injury or loss of oxygen in the first minutes of life), or early neonatal factors (being a premature baby with difficulty of maintaining temperature, breathing, and having intestinal difficulties) or early development trauma (severe accidental burns or need for operations). All of these many factors might have destroyed the infant's basic trust (Erikson, 1950) in the world, producing very demanding and difficult behavior and actions for the mother to handle. For some mothers, there may be no good solution or method for protecting the growing young child from life's harsher experiences.

Teachers must be very careful in early childhood centers and schools not to make harsh value judgments and assign blame to mothers and fathers. The negative behavior that a child exhibits might have been far beyond the parent's abilities and sphere of skill to manage and handle. But if a teacher sees a cycle of negative parent-child interaction, such as abuse, she should take all necessary steps to encourage parents to enroll in parenting skill classes or obtain the counseling of child experts and professionals.

Reconsider Mrs. Waffle, who may, without outside help, become a punitive, noneffective parent. The teacher can help by encouraging her to assess her personality core with the use of the Parents' Beliefs about Discipline (Guidance) Inventory (see Figure 8.1). This model permits her to stop waffling, create orderliness to her behavior, and move away from punishment and excessive controlling behaviors, which will in turn enable her child to understand her actions. Thus she becomes predictable and effective with her child.

Parent Guidance Books and Models

The suggested materials presented in Appendix A to help parents do not include "here today, gone tomorrow" models and books but focus on those guidance models that are based on solid psychological theory and have stood the test of time. They are classified under the three philosophy models (relationship-listening, confronting-contracting, and rules-rewards) used to characterize a parent's response to the Parents' Beliefs about Discipline (Guidance) Inventory (see Figure 8.1).

Relationship-Listening: A relationship-listening model, such as Parent Effectiveness Training (Gordon, 1974, 1988), uses minimum control and views the child as having the capacity to change his own behavior. According to this model, a child acts out in an aggressive manner because of emotional turmoil or flooded feelings. The goal of the P.E.T. model is to make the child aware of his actions and to get him to talk out his emotional concerns. This talking it out by the child leads the child to become more purposeful in his behavior. The parenting techniques of the relationship-listening model emphasize minimal intervention, such as active listening and problem solving, and they reject the use of time-out and other forms of praise, rewards, or punishment.

Confronting-Contracting: The confronting-contracting model, represented by Dreikurs (1964), is one in which the difficult child is granted the power to decide how he will change. The parent encourages and contracts with the child to live up to a mutual agreement for behavioral change. The confronting-contracting position primarily sees the child as being motivated by an excessive need for attention, power, or feelings of revenge or helplessness. The parent then takes steps to give the child power and attention in an acceptable way through encouraging behaviors. Punishment is not suggested, but the parent does learn to use logical consequences and sanctions related to misdeeds, to help the child learn the consequences of his actions.

Rules-Consequences: The rules-consequences philosophy communicates, "This is the rule and behavior that I want. I will reward new positive behaviors acquired by the child." The parent defines small positive changes that she seeks, rewarding these changes so that they will be repeated. The parent also uses some forms of negative sanctions, such as time-out, but general punishment is not used.

With the understanding of the three large philosophical approaches to child guidance and discipline—relationship-listening, confronting-contracting, and rules-rewards—and with the use of the Parents' Beliefs about Discipline (Guidance) Inventory, the teacher is now in the position to suggest that the parent acquire new knowledge by reading books, watching videos, or seeking training in these models.

Other Guidance Initiatives

Parent Workshops or Education Groups: The teacher may survey all parents to determine what topics are of interest to them. Parent workshops or meetings can range from one three-hour session to a monthlong series of meetings on a particular subject. Parents should be grouped with regard to their philosophical orientation. Meetings can be offered periodically or whenever a need arises. Topics may include child development, discipline and behavior issues, or other topics that may interest parents. Teachers either can lead sessions or invite an outside expert to speak. (Appendix B presents Internet Resources for Parents.)

Parent Resource Room or Lending Library: A small bookshelf or separate room or closet can be dedicated to display and store books and videotapes that would be helpful to parents. With a simple system established for checking out resources, parents would be able to take the resources home to read or view. Some schools have extended this idea to other resources, such as children's board games, puzzles, and building blocks, which parents can also check out to use at home with their children for a given period of time.

Parent-Teacher Conferences: Parent and teacher conferences provide a valuable source of information and an opportunity for personal communication. These are usually scheduled at least twice a year to share developmental information and insights concerning the child's growth. Additional conferences may be scheduled at the parents' request or as a teacher deems necessary. Work samples, photographs, and anecdotal notes can help parents understand changes in the child's development.

Here are some teacher guidelines for the parent-teacher conference:

1. Be prepared for the conference. Gather all information available concerning the child.
2. Begin and end the conference on a positive note. If there is a concern to be communicated, it is best done in the middle of the conference.
3. Allow time and encourage parents to ask questions or share information concerning their child.
4. Help parents come to solutions to problems that really belong to them. Gordon (1974) explains the concept of problem ownership.

5. Conferences should be held at a convenient time for parents. Allow for privacy and, if possible, provide child care for siblings so parents can attend the conference without the responsibility of caring for children.
6. Stay on schedule so that other parents who are waiting for a conference time are not inconvenienced.
7. At the end of the conference, summarize the agreements made, write them down, and put them in the child's folder.
8. If necessary, share information from the conference with other school personnel, support services, special education personnel, etc.

Home Visits: Home visits allow teachers to obtain valuable information about the child and home environment, meet the family, and learn how to support the child's transition to school. Some teachers visit the home of each child enrolled in their class at the beginning of the school year; however, home visits can be done at any time during the year. The teacher should be sensitive to parents by writing a note or making a phone call to request a specific time to visit and allow parents to refuse a home visit.

Informal Parent-Teacher Discussion: When a parent picks up a child at the end of the day, the brief teacher-parent verbal exchange presents a critical opportunity to reassure parents and share information, successes, or concerns related to the child's experiences that day. One teacher, normally the lead teacher, should be available to speak with parents during the first hour in the morning and the last hour at the end of the day.

Summary

Helping parents to help their difficult child may mean directing them to resources for guidance and discipline. Teachers can assess the parents' philosophical beliefs related to guidance and discipline and help them find resources that will be meaningful to them. A wide variety of parent-school-classroom activities also can be used to set the stage for positive communication and working relationships between the teacher and parents.

REFERENCES

Dreikurs, R. (1964). *Children: The challenge.* New York: E. P. Dutton.
Erikson, E. H. (1950). *Childhood and society.* New York: W. W. Norton.
Escalona, S. (1968). *The roots of individuality.* Chicago: Aldine Publishing.
Gordon, T. (1974). *Parent effectiveness training: P.E.T.* New York: Peter H. Wyden Publishing.
Gordon, T. (1988). *Teaching children self-discipline: At home and at school.* New York: Times Books.
Piaget, J. (1965). *The moral judgement of the child.* New York: Free Press.

Parent Books and Resources

Rules-Rewards

Becker, W. C. (1971). *Parents are teachers.* Champaign, Ill: Research Press.

Canter, L., & Canter, M. (1985). *Assertive discipline for parents.* (rev. ed.). New York: Harper & Row.

Christopherson, E. R. (1977). *Little people: Guidelines for common sense rearing.* Lawrence, KS: H & H Enterprises.

*Forehand, R., & Long, N. (2002). *Parenting the strong-willed child.* Chicago: Contemporary Books.

Levy, R., & O'Hanlon, B., with Goode, T. N. (2001). *Try and make me: Simple strategies that turn off the tantrums and create cooperation.* Emmaus, PA: Rodale.

Macht, J. (1975). *Teaching our children.* New York: John Wiley and Sons.

Madsen, C. K., & Madsen, C. H. (1970). *Parents-children-discipline: A positive approach.* Boston: Allyn and Bacon.

Phelan, T. (1995). *1–2–3 Magic: Effective discipline for children 2–12.* Glen Ellyn, IL: Child Management.

Retig, E. B. (1973). *ABC's for parents.* Van Nuys, CA: Association for Behavior Change.

*Sears, W. & Sears, M. (1995). *The discipline book: How to have a better-behaved child: From birth to age ten.* Boston: Little, Brown.

Severe, S. (2000). *How to behave so your children will, too!* New York: Viking.

Waggonseller, B. R., Burnett, M., Salzberg, B., & Burnett, J. (1977). *The art of parenting: Communication; assertion training; behavior management; motivation: behavior management: Methods; behavior management: discipline.* Champaign, Ill: Research Press.

Wenning, K. (1996). *Winning cooperation from you child: A comprehensive method to stop defiant and aggressive behavior in children.* Northvale, NJ: Jason Aronson.

Confronting-Contracting

Albert, L. (1989). *Teacher's guide to cooperative discipline: How to manage your classroom and promote self-esteem.* Circle Pines, MN: American Guidance Service.

Dinkmeyer, D., & Dreikurs, R. (1963). *Encouraging children to learn: The encouragement process.* Upper Saddle River, NJ: Prentice Hall.

*Recommended

Dinkmeyer, D., & McKay, G. (1996). *Raising a responsible child* (rev. ed.). New York: Fireside.

Dinkmeyer, D., McKay, G., & Dinkmeyer, D. (1997). *The parent's handbook.* Circle Pines, MN: American Guidance Service.

Dinkmeyer, D., McKay, G., Dinkmeyer, J., & Dinkmeyer, D. (1997). *Early childhood STEP.* Circle Pines, MN: American Guidance Service.

*Dreikurs, R. (1964). *Children: The challenge.* New York: E. P. Dutton.

Dreikurs, R., & Cassel, P. (1972). *Discipline without tears: What to do with children who misbehave* (rev. ed.). New York: Hawthorn Books.

Dreikurs, R., & Loren, G. (1968). *Logical consequences.* New York: Meredith Press.

*MacKenzie, R. J. (1998). *Setting limits: How to raise responsible, independent children by providing clear boundaries.* Roseville, CA: Prima Publishing.

Nelson, J., Duffy, R. Escobar, L., Ortolano, K., & Owen-Sohocki, D. (1996). *Positive discipline: A teacher's A-Z guide.* Roseville, CA: Prima Publishing.

Tayler, J. F. (2001). *From defiance to cooperation: Real solutions for transforming the angry, defiant, discouraged child.* Roseville, CA: Prima Publishing.

Relationship-Listening

Bailey, B. (2000). *Conscious discipline.* Oviedo, FL: Loving Guidance.

Faber, A., & Mazlish, E. (1974). *Liberated parents, liberated children.* New York: Avon.

*Faber, A., & Mazlish, E. (1980). *How to talk so kids will listen and listen so kids will talk.* New York: Avon.

*Gordon, T. (1974). *Parent effectiveness training: P.E.T.* New York: Peter H. Wyden Publishing.

Gordon, T. (1988). *Teaching children self-discipline: At home and at school.* New York: Times Books.

Greenspan, S. L. (1995). *The challenging child: Understanding, raising, and enjoying the five "different" types of children.* Cambridge, MA: Perseus Books.

*Spears, D. S., & Braund, R. L. (1996). *Strong-willed child or dreamer.* Nashville: Thomas Nelson Publishers.

Internet Resources for Parents

Center for Effective Parenting
www.parent-ed.org
The "Parent Handouts" section gives information on handling difficult situations.

Child and Family WebGuide
www.cfw.fufts.edu
This Web site links parents to other Web sites related to research and parenting.

Connecting with Kids
www.connectingwithkids.com
This Web site provides information related to health and behavioral issues for children at home and at school.

Family Literacy Web Sites and Resourses
www.literacy.owcc.net/famli/parents/discipline.htm
Deals with discipline, school concerns, parenting skills, family reference book, and a host of materials related to literacy.

KidsSource Online
www.kidsource.com
Parenting, health, education, and recreation information is provided.

National Parent Information Network
www.npin.org
Parents can submit questions that will appear at a later time with suggestions in the *Parent News* letter. Books for parents also are reviewed.

ParentCenter
www.parentcenter.com
Especially designed for parents with two- to eight-year-olds, and focuses on difficulties related to this age group.

Parenting Resources for the 21st Century

www.parentingresource.ncjrs.org

This Web site links to a host of other sites related to raising children, developmental, society, and school issues.

ParentPlace

www.parentsplace.com

Provides question-and-answer sessions with parenting and child experts as well as a chat room.

Parent Soup

www.parentsoup.com

Parents get suggestions as well as discussion and chat groups offering the opportunity to talk to experts.

Practical Parenting

www.practicalparent.org.uk

This United Kingdom Web site provides practical advice to parents, including an offer for a free publication, called *The Practical Parenting Newsletter*.

QualKids

www.qualkids.com

This Web site is for child-care providers.

Tigerchild

www.tigerchild.com

This United Kingdom Web site deals with child development and parenting issues.

INDEX